HORS D'OEUVRES EVERYBODY LOVES II

More Party Menus with Recipes to Win Your Heart

To my dear friend Mana with love and best wishes for happy cooking —

Mary Leigh Furrh

Authors Jo Barksdale (left) and Mary Leigh Furrh.

Hors D'Oeuvres Everybody Loves II

PARTY MENUS WITH RECIPES
TO WIN YOUR HEART

by Mary Leigh Furrh
and Jo Barksdale

QUAIL RIDGE PRESS

Dedicated to Jim Furrh, Mary Leigh's husband,
for his encouragement and support,
and to Shirley Tate, whose tireless efforts helped
make this book a reality.

Library of Congress Cataloging-in-Publication Data

Furrh, Mary Leigh.
    Hors d'oeuvres everybody loves II: party menus with recipes to
win your heart / by Mary Leigh Furrh and Jo Barksdale.
      p. cm.
    ISBN 0-937552-91-7
    1. Appetizers. 2. Entertaining. 3. Menus. I. Barksdale, Jr.
II. Title.
TX740.F87 1998
641.8' 12--dc21   98-39324
                                      CIP

CONTENTS

PREFACE

Everybody loves hors d'oeuvres. If a pollster asked every cook in the United States to name the food category he or she prepares most, hors d'oeuvres would win, hands down. Occasions for serving hors d'oeuvres arise constantly—a glass of wine and a dip shared with your next-door neighbor, a cup of tea and a finger sandwich enjoyed with your favorite cousin—as well as those eagerly anticipated teas and cocktail parties where you catch up on everyone's news.

Since we wrote Hors D'Oeuvres Everybody Loves in 1983, the food world has been re-invented many times, but the book is still a popular seller. Its success proves that good recipes stand the test of time.

During the past 15 years, however, we have collected a wide variety of new recipes that beg to be shared. Many reflect the trends of the late eighties and nineties. Ethnic and fusion cuisines have emerged, and we have included examples such as Outback Biscuits and Mildred Brown's Quesadillas. Fast, easy-does-it methods are popular, so we shared a lot of quick appetizers like Sausage Balls with Jezebel Sauce and Alice's Festive Bean Dip.

We proudly credit our friends who shared their recipes (towns are all in Mississippi unless otherwise noted), and we gave the number of servings whenever possible. But sometimes this depends on the variety of items on the menu and the hour of the party. The origins of the recipes given to us by friends were not always possible to find, although we tried hard to trace them. As a recipe travels from cook to cook with each adding a special touch, there is often no way to determine its original source.

Marvelous food will make your party memorable, but no one will have fun unless you enjoy it, too. Our recipes are easy, and most can be done ahead, leaving you free to mingle. So, relax, and keep in mind that being well-organized and genuinely caring about your guests are the most important items on the menu. Above all, remember that a sense of humor is more essential than salt and pepper.

Jo Barksdale and Mary Leigh Furrh

HEARTWARMING COCKTAIL BUFFETS

Mucho Gusto! It's a Southwestern Fiesta

Come for a Casual Cocktail Supper

We're Having a Christmas Eve Celebration

It's a New Year's Eve Party— New Orleans Style

Our cocktail buffet menus were designed to serve as small meals. We turned entrées into hors d'oeuvres, to show their versatility, in dishes like Curried Shrimp and Shrimp Creole Risotto. Then we added filling meat recipes for Pork Tenderloin Tequila, Glazed Turkey Breasts with Raspberry Sauce, and many others.

Savory cheesecakes have come into their own and have the added feature of serving a large crowd without replenishing. A presentation of three flavors, as we used in the "Come for a Casual Cocktail Supper" menu, is practical as well as eye-catching.

We balanced the meat and cheese dishes with lighter vegetable specialties such as Asparagus with Lemon Yogurt Dip and Guacamole Mold with Crudités. Then, best of all, we included fruit recipes like Pears with Caramel Fondue and Chocolate Orange Sauce with Fresh Fruit followed by yummy sweets such as Bravo's Cappuccino Brownies and Cranberry Pecan Tassies.

Mucho Gusto! It's a Southwestern Fiesta

Pork Tenderloin Tequila
Martha's Sausage Cheese Tartlets
Quesadilla Pie
Guacamole Mold with Crudités
Alice's Festive Bean Dip
Pears with Caramel Fondue
Bravo's Cappuccino Brownies

Pork Tenderloin Tequila
Tangy taste contrasts with rest of menu

2 (3-pound) pork tenderloins	¼ cup lime juice
1 cup tequila	½ cup fresh rosemary,
1½ cups vegetable oil	chopped
1 teaspoon black pepper	3 cloves of garlic, minced
1 teaspoon seasoning salt	¾ teaspoon cumin
2 teaspoons sugar	

Place tenderloins in baking dish. Mix remaining ingredients and pour over them. Marinate in refrigerator overnight. Remove pork to another dish, saving marinade. Place in pre-heated 400° oven to brown 5 minutes. Reduce heat to 350° and roast until oven thermometer reaches 165°, basting every ten minutes with marinade. Serve on platter, sliced and garnished with rosemary sprigs. Place basket of whole wheat rolls nearby and a dish of Jezebel sauce for guests to make sandwiches. (Jezebel sauce on page 62).

Martha's Sausage Cheese Tartlets
Easy to serve—fun to eat

2 cups cooked sausage, drained on paper towels and crumbled
1½ cups grated sharp cheddar cheese
1½ cups grated Monterey Jack cheese
1 package ranch-style dressing mix
1 (4½-ounce) can chopped black olives
½ cup finely chopped red bell pepper
1 package won ton wrappers, cut into quarters
Olive oil

For filling, combine sausage, cheeses, dressing mix, olives and bell pepper in large bowl and mix well.

Lightly rub miniature muffin tins with olive oil. Press won ton wrapper in each cup and lightly brush wrapper with oil. Bake 5 minutes at 350° until golden. Remove wrappers from tins and transfer to baking sheet. Fill wrappers with sausage mixture. Bake 10 minutes at 350° or until bubbly and heated through. Makes 4–5 dozen.

Quesadilla Pie
Cumin adds to Southwestern flavor

2 (4-ounce) cans green-chilies, chopped and drained
4 cups Monterey Jack cheese, grated
1 teaspoon cumin
2 cups milk (may use skim)
1 cup baking mix
4 eggs
Lowfat sour cream, salsa, guacamole

Spray a 9x13-inch glass dish with no-stick cooking spray. Sprinkle chilies and cheese on bottom. Blend together cumin, milk, baking mix and eggs in mixer; beat until smooth. Pour into dish.

Preheat oven to 375° and bake mixture 30–35 minutes or until toothpick inserted between center and edge comes out clean. Let stand until cool. Slice into squares. Top each square with a teaspoon of sour cream. Top sour cream with alternate dabs of salsa and guacamole. Makes approximately 24. For a small group, divide recipe in half and bake in 8-inch pie plate. Cut into wedges, top with condiments, and serve with a fork on individual salad plates. Serves 8.

Guacamole Mold with Crudités

An unusual presentation for fresh vegetables

3 envelopes unflavored
    gelatin
½ cup cold water
½ cup hot water
2 ripe avocados (about 2
    pounds)
2 tablespoons chopped mild
    green chilies
2 tablespoons lemon juice
1 teaspoon salt
½ teaspoon cumin

2 cloves garlic, chopped
1 tablespoon Worcestershire
    sauce
1 (8-ounces) packages cream
    cheese, softened
Salsa (optional)
Fresh vegetables, crisped
    (carrot sticks, broccoli and
    cauliflower florets, cherry
    tomatoes)

Sprinkle gelatin over cold water in small bowl; soften for 5 minutes. Add hot water, stirring to dissolve gelatin. Refrigerate until cool. Cut avocado into chunks and drop into food processor. Combine with chilies and lemon juice. Blend, just to make a smooth purée. Add salt, cumin, garlic, Worcestershire sauce, cream cheese and cooled gelatin. Blend to combine ingredients. Turn into a 4-cup greased mold. Refrigerate at least 4 hours until firm.

Unmold and surround with chilled vegetables. May drizzle salsa over mold if desired. May also serve with boiled shrimp.

Alice's Festive Bean Dip

Soul satisfying comfort food with punch

2 cups cheddar cheese,
    shredded
1 (16-ounce) can black
    beans, drained and
    mashed
1 (8-ounce) can corn kernels
1 cup Mexican tomatoes,
    mashed

1 small jar salsa (medium or
    hot)
1 (8-ounce) carton sour
    cream
1 cup black olives, sliced
1 cup Mozzarella cheese,
    shredded

Preheat oven to 400°. Combine first 6 ingredients in a 2-quart casserole. Sprinkle with onions, olives and cheese. Cover and bake 15–20 minutes. Uncover and bake 15 additional minutes until bubbly. Serve with tortilla chips.

Pears with Caramel Fondue

You may serve the sauce over ice cream or pound cake

**12 firm-ripe Anjou, Bosc and
Bartlett Pears, unpeeled**

**2 quarts ice water
3 tablespoons Fruit-Fresh**

Ripen pears at room temperature until mellow. Cut into cubes. Submerge them in ice water to which Fruit-Fresh has been added. Soak 1–2 minutes and drain. Dry on paper towels

Caramel Fondue:

**1 cup margarine, melted
2 cups dark brown sugar
¾ cup light corn syrup
1 (14-ounce) can sweetened
condensed milk**

**¼ teaspoon salt
½ cup light cream
1 teaspoon vanilla**

Mix together first 5 ingredients in the top of a double boiler. Place over barely simmering water and cook 1 hour, stirring occasionally and keeping water level low. Stir in cream and vanilla and cook 30 more minutes. Cool and refrigerate. Bring to room temperature and heat slightly before serving in a bowl with unpeeled pear cubes around base for dipping. Place toothpicks nearby.

Bravo's Cappuccino Brownies

Much-requested recipe from a Jackson restaurant

**1 cup unsalted butter
12-ounces semisweet chocolate chips
2 teaspoons instant
cappuccino or espresso
powders
½ teaspoon cinnamon**

**5 eggs
1½ cups sugar
1 1/8 cups flour
½ cup bittersweet chocolate,
chopped
Confectioners' sugar**

Melt butter and semisweet chocolate chips in the top of a double boiler over low heat until smooth. Stir in instant cappuccino or espresso and cinnamon. In a large bowl, combine eggs and sugar. Mix in chocolate mixture, and slowly fold in flour. Finally, fold in chopped bittersweet chocolate. Pour batter into an 8x12-inch pan that has been lined with buttered and floured foil. Bake in the lower third of a 350° oven for about 30 minutes or until a cake tester comes out clean. Cool. Lift out foil with brownies on it. Cut them into 2½x2½-inch squares. Cut squares into triangles. Sift confectioners' sugar over brownies. Makes 48 triangles.

Come for a Casual Cocktail Supper

Beef Tenderloin with Horseradish Sauce
Curried Shrimp Dip with Toast Cups
Caponata on Polenta Rounds
Asparagus with Lemon Yogurt Dip
Cheesecake Presentation (Stilton
Cheesecake, Artichoke Cheesecake
and Salmon Cheesecake)
Chocolate Zucchini Cookies
Apricot Squares

Beef Tenderloin with Horseradish Sauce

An elegant anchor for your cocktail buffet

½ cup olive oil
¼ cup Worcestershire sauce
¼ cup soy sauce
½ cup red wine
2 cloves garlic, minced
1 teaspoon freshly ground pepper
1 teaspoon seasoned salt
¼ cup lemon juice
4 to 6-pound beef tenderloin, trimmed
Kitchen Bouquet
Rolls

Combine first 8 ingredients. Place beef in marinade and refrigerate at least 4 hours. Remove from refrigerator an hour before cooking. Preheat oven to 450°. Transfer tenderloin to a clean pan. Rub with Kitchen Bouquet. Cook for 35 minutes for medium rare. Serve with rolls and Horseradish Sauce.

HORSERADISH SAUCE:

1 cup mayonnaise
2 tablespoons horseradish
Dash Tabasco
1 teaspoon Worcestershire

Combine all ingredients and chill.

Curried Shrimp Dip with Toast Cups

A popular entrée transformed into an hors d'oeuvre

**2 tablespoons butter or
  margarine**
**1½ cups finely chopped
  apples**
2 tablespoons flour
**2–2½ teaspoons curry
  powder**

2 cups milk
1 teaspoon salt
**2–3 cups cooked, cleaned
  shrimp, chopped**
**Chutney, chopped peanuts,
  coconut, pickle relish**
Toast Cups (page 21)

Melt butter; add apples and cook 5 minutes. Stir flour and curry powder into apples. Add milk slowly. Cook until sauce thickens, stirring constantly. Add salt. Stir in shrimp and heat thoroughly. Place in chafing dish. Serve chutney, chopped peanuts, coconut and pickle relish in small bowls for condiments. Serve with Toast Cups.

Caponata

A healthy appetizer from Sicily

**1 clove of garlic, peeled and
  chopped**
Olive oil
2 onions, diced
**2 eggplants, peeled, sliced,
  salted, drained, and diced**
**1 medium red bell pepper,
  peeled and diced**
**1 medium green bell pepper,
  peeled and diced**
3 tablespoons pine nuts
⅓ cup fresh basil, chopped
2 tablespoons capers

**1 (28-ounce) can plum
  tomatoes, drained,
  seeded, chopped**
2 tablespoons sugar
**1–2 tablespoons Balsamic
  vinegar**
1 tablespoon tomato paste
½ teaspoon seasoning salt
Polenta Rounds
**Approximately 6 table-
  spoons shredded
  Parmesan cheese**

Sauté garlic in olive oil until golden, add onions and cook until translucent. Stir in eggplant, adding more oil to prevent sticking. Add red and green peppers and sauté until tender. Mix in pine nuts, basil, and capers. Stir in tomatoes, sugar, vinegar, tomato paste and seasoning salt. Chill overnight in refrigerator. Place on polenta rounds and top with shredded Parmesan cheese. Bake in 350° oven for 10–12 minutes. Serve immediately. Caponata may also be served cold on crostini.

Polenta Rounds

Top with any spicy mixture

6 cups water
2 cups yellow cornmeal
2 teaspoons salt

2 cups cold water
½ cup freshly grated
   Parmesan cheese

Bring 6 cups water to a boil. Mix cornmeal, salt and 2 cups cold water in a bowl. Slowly add cornmeal mixture to boiling water, stirring constantly. Cook and stir until mixture comes to a boil. Reduce heat to low. Cook 10–15 minutes or until thick, stirring occasionally. Stir in Parmesan.

Pour into 2 lightly greased 15x10x1-inch baking pans. Cool 1 hour; chill until firm. Refrigerate 2–3 days. Cut circles from polenta, using a small round cutter. Yield: 5 dozen.

Stilton Cheesecake

Rich and velvety texture, enhanced with walnuts

¼ cup grated Parmesan
   cheese
¼ cup fine dry bread crumbs
1 tablespoon butter
1¾ pounds cream cheese,
   room temperature

½ pound Stilton cheese
⅓ cup heavy cream
4 eggs
1½ cups chopped walnuts,
   toasted

Preheat oven to 325°. Mix together Parmesan and bread crumbs. Use butter to grease a 9-inch springform pan. Sprinkle bread crumb mixture over bottom of pan.

Mix cream cheese in mixer. Blend in crumbled Stilton and cream. Beat in eggs, one at a time. Stir in 1 cup toasted walnuts. Pour into springform pan. Set pan in larger pan and fill halfway up the sides with hot water. Bake 1 hour and 20 minutes. Turn off oven and cool cheesecake with door ajar for 1 hour. Cool to room temperature and remove from springform pan. Top with remaining toasted walnuts. Serve with crackers.

Strawberry Fans: Hold strawberries on a cutting surface and make parallel cuts from the tips of berries to as close to the stem as possible without cutting through. Press berry gently to fan slices.

Asparagus and Lemon Yogurt Dip

Low in fat, high in flavor

4 pounds thin asparagus
1 cup lemon yogurt
1 teaspoon lemon rind,
grated

1 teaspoon dried dill
2 teaspoons fresh chives,
chopped

Blanch asparagus in large pan of boiling water for 3 minutes. Drain. Plunge into cold water to cool. Drain and pat dry with dish towel. Refrigerate, wrapped in plastic wrap.

For sauce: stir together lemon yogurt, rind, dill and chives. Refrigerate. Serve dip in a small bowl surrounded by asparagus spears.

Charlotte's Artichoke Cheesecake

This rich, creamy spread serves a crowd easily

4 tablespoons butter
¼ cup (approximately)
Italian bread crumbs
1 (15-ounce) can artichoke
hearts, drained
½ cup Italian dressing made
with olive oil
3 (8-ounce) packages cream
cheese, softened
1½ cups feta cheese,
crumbled

1½ teaspoons fresh
oregano, chopped
¼ teaspoon garlic powder
3 large eggs
½ cup chopped green on-
ions, including tops
1 teaspoon grated lemon
rind
Fresh basil leaves

Preheat oven to 325°. Butter sides and bottom of a 9-inch springform pan. Sprinkle bread crumbs into pan, tilting it to be sure sides and bottom are covered with crumbs.

Drain and chop artichoke hearts. Marinate in Italian dressing 4 hours or overnight, setting aside 2 tablespoons of marinade. Beat cream cheese, feta, oregano, and garlic powder in a large bowl. Add eggs, beating until just blended. Do not overbeat. Add drained artichokes, the 2 tablespoons of marinade, green onions and lemon rind. After combining well, pour the mixture into the springform pan lined with crumbs. Cover loosely with foil. Bake 35–40 minutes or until sides are firm when shaken. Cool. Chill for at least 2 hours and up to 24 hours. Remove from pan and garnish with basil leaves. Serve at room temperature.

Make the Salmon Cheesecake on page 18. Place the three cheesecakes on cake stands and arrange them with a bowlful of crackers in the middle.

Chocolate Zucchini Cookies

From The Sanders—Helena's Bed and Breakfast, Helena, Montana

½ cup margarine, softened
½ cup vegetable oil
1¾ cup sugar
2 eggs
½ teaspoon vanilla
½ cup sour milk*
4 cups flour
4 tablespoons cocoa

½ teaspoon baking powder
1 teaspoon baking soda
½ teaspoon cinnamon
½ teaspoon cloves
2 cups finely diced zucchini
12-ounces semisweet chocolate chips

Cream margarine, oil and sugar. Add eggs and vanilla, and combine thoroughly. Beat sour milk into margarine mixture. Mix dry ingredients well and add to the creamed mixture. Beat well again. Stir in zucchini and chocolate chips. Spoon onto a greased cookie sheet and bake about 12 minutes at 350°. Cookies should have a cake-like texture and not spread too much. Makes 12 dozen small cookies.

*Make sour milk by adding 1 teaspoon lemon juice or vinegar to milk and letting it stand 5 minutes.

Apricot Squares

Delicate almond and apricot pastries

½ cup margarine
½ cup sugar
2 eggs, separated
1 teaspoon coconut
    amaretto (or ½ teaspoon
    almond extract)
1½ cups flour, sifted

½ teaspoon baking powder
¼ teaspoon salt
¼ teaspoon baking soda
1 (18-ounce) jar apricot
    preserves
¾ cup sliced almonds

Cream margarine and sugar in mixer. Beat in egg yolks. Add coconut amaretto or almond extract. Sift together dry ingredients and add gradually to mixture. Pat into a well-oiled 9x13-inch pan. Smooth preserves over top, then sprinkle half of the almonds over the preserves. Beat egg whites and spread thinly over mixture. Scatter remaining almonds over all. Bake in preheated 350° oven for approximately 40 minutes. Cool in pan; chill one hour before cutting into 2-inch squares. Store in refrigerator. Makes 36–40 squares.

We're Having a Christmas Eve Celebration

Raspberry Orange Glazed Turkey
Breast with Raspberry Sauce
Salmon Cheese Cake with Salmon Roe
Mack's Oyster Rockefeller
Mushrooms in Toast Cups
Asparagus Mousse with Crudites
Sweet Potato Biscuits, Ham and
Chutney Butter
Chocolate Orange Sauce with
Fresh Fruit
Cranberry Pecan Tassies

Raspberry Orange Glazed Turkey Breast

A jewel in a cook's crown

1 (2-pound) turkey breast
roast
1 cup orange juice
1 teaspoon ground sage
½ teaspoon thyme leaves
½ teaspoon pepper

½ teaspoon salt
1 teaspoon orange peel,
grated
2 cups fresh or frozen
raspberries (unthawed)
⅓ cup sugar

Defrost turkey breast, if frozen, according to package directions. Preheat oven to 350°. Pour orange juice over turkey that has been placed in a shallow baking pan. Sprinkle with herbs, pepper, salt and orange peel. Bake, basting occasionally, for 1 hour and 20 minutes. Combine raspberries and sugar. Place around the turkey breast. Continue baking 10 or 15 minutes or until thermometer registers done. Remove from oven and spoon some of the berries over the turkey. Let stand 10 minutes before slicing. Cranberries may be substituted for raspberries. Will serve 8 for dinner or 16 for cocktails.

Serve with Raspberry Sauce, butter, and small thin slices of bread. To serve completely sliced; scatter the raspberries around and in between rows of turkey slices. Serve sauce warm in a separate bowl. Serve butter in a separate bowl.

Raspberry Sauce

This sweet-sour, ruby red sauce also compliments pork

1 (10-ounce) package red
  raspberries, thawed
2 tablespoons dry white
  wine
1 tablespoon orange liqueur

2 teaspoons cornstarch
1 tablespoons butter or
  margarine

Purée raspberries in food processor until smooth. Combine wine, orange liqueur, and cornstarch. Stir in raspberries and butter. Cook and stir over medium low heat until thickened and bubbly. Cook 2 minutes and stir 2 additional minutes. Sieve. Serve warm. Makes 1¼ cups sauce.

Salmon Cheese Cake with Salmon Roe

Garnish with sour cream and salmon roe

½ cup cracker crumbs
3 (8-ounce) packages cream
  cheese, softened
½ cup light cream
¼ cup butter, softened
2 teaspoons prepared mus-
  tard
½ teaspoon dill weed
¼ teaspoon salt
¼ teaspoon red pepper
4 eggs

1 (14½-ounce) can red
  Sockeye salmon, drained,
  skin and bones removed
1 (8-ounce) package natural
  aged Swiss cheese, shredded
1 bunch green onions, finely
  chopped
1 (8-ounce) carton sour
  cream
2 (2-ounce) jars salmon roe
  or red caviar

Preheat oven to 450°. Butter a springform pan generously. Coat bottom and sides with crumbs.

Beat cream cheese, cream, butter, mustard, dill, salt and red pepper until well blended. Add eggs, one at a time, mixing well after each addition.

Add salmon, Swiss cheese and onions, mixing at low speed with mixer until well blended. Pour over crumbs. Bake 10 minutes. Reduce oven to 250°; continue baking 1 hour or until it tests done with a straw. Loosen from rim of pan with a knife. Cool before removing rim of pan.

Chill. Garnish before serving by spreading sour cream over the top and covering sour cream with salmon roe or red caviar. Serve with water crackers or toasted French bread slices.

Mack's Oyster Rockefeller

A Christmas Eve tradition passed down
from the McDonnell family of Hazelhurst

¼ **bunch celery, chopped**
1 **bunch green onions, chopped**
1 **(2-ounce) can anchovies, chopped**
¼ **bunch parsley, minced**
4 **(10-ounces) boxes spinach, undrained, thawed**
¼ **cup butter, softened**
½ **teaspoon liquid crab boil**
Juice of 1 large lemon
¼ **teaspoon Creole seasoning salt, or to taste**
4–6 **drops Tabasco sauce, or to taste**

¼ **teaspoon garlic salt, or to taste**
2–3 **tablespoons Worcestershire sauce, or to taste**
½ **cup plain bread crumbs (approximately)**
½ **cup Italian bread crumbs (approximately)**
¼ **cup Herbsaint or Pernod liqueur, or to taste**
3 **or 4 dozen oysters (smaller ones are best)**
8 **pie pans**
3 **pounds ice cream salt**

Makes 2 quarts topping. Freezes well. Blend celery, onions and anchovies together until almost a paste. Mix with parsley, spinach with juice, and butter. Cook over low heat, stirring often. Season with crab boil, lemon, Creole seasoning, Tabasco, garlic salt and Worcestershire sauce to taste. Mix bread crumbs together, adding a little at the time to thicken the mixture to desired consistency. Not too dry! Add Herbsaint or Pernod to taste.

Drain oysters and shells, well. Partially fill pie pans with ice cream salt. Place oysters in shells on salt (6 to a pan). Cook oysters under broiler until the edges begin to curl. Drain off liquid. Spoon hot Rockefeller sauce on top and run under the broiler again until slightly browned.

Oysters may also be served from a chafing dish. Heat sauce. Drain oysters well and remove from the shells. Place in a single layer in a shallow pan. Bake at 400° until edges curl, about 5 or 6 minutes. Transfer them to a chafing dish and combine with heated sauce.

Mushrooms in Toast Cups
Delicious little tarts—make in quantity and freeze

TOAST CUPS:

24 thin slices white bread

3 tablespoons butter, softened

Cut 3-inch rounds from bread. Brush 2 miniature muffin pans generously with butter. Fit rounds gently into each cup. Bake 10 minutes, until lightly browned, in a preheated 400° oven. Makes 24 toast cups.

FILLING:

3 tablespoons green onions, finely chopped
¼ cup butter
½ pound fresh mushrooms, finely chopped
2 tablespoons flour
1 cup heavy cream
1½ tablespoons chives, finely chopped

1 tablespoon parsley, finely chopped
½ teaspoon lemon juice
½ teaspoon salt
⅛ teaspoon cayenne pepper
2 tablespoons Parmesan cheese, grated
2 teaspoons parsley, chopped
Butter

Sauté onions in butter for 1 minute. Stir in mushrooms. Simmer uncovered until liquid evaporates. Remove from heat and stir in flour. Pour cream over mixture and return to heat. Bring to a boil, stirring constantly. Cook until thick (about 1 minute). Stir in remaining ingredients except for cheese, parsley and butter. Let cool, cover and refrigerate.

Spoon mixture into Toast Cups. You may freeze at this point. Thaw before baking.

Preheat oven to 350°. Sprinkle with cheese and parsley. Place on an ungreased baking sheet. Dot with slivers of butter. Bake 10 minutes. If desired, you may then run under a broiler for quick browning.

Tip: Freeze food in their baking containers, covered. When frozen, remove from container and place in a heavy plastic bag.

 For an hors d'oeuvre cheese tray, furnish several small dishes of herbs and spices to dip cheese cubes. Try freshly ground black pepper, chopped dill, parsley or thyme.

Asparagus Mousse with Crudites

Regal on the buffet table

1 ½ tablespoons gelatin
¼ cup cold water
1 cup asparagus liquid
2 (10-ounce) cans green
    asparagus
1 cup mayonnaise
1 large lemon
1 cup heavy cream, whipped

1 teaspoon onion juice, or
    3–4 tablespoons onion,
    finely chopped
1 teaspoon Worcestershire
    sauce
⅛ teaspoon salt, or to taste
⅛ teaspoon red pepper, or to
    taste

Soak gelatin in cold water. Heat asparagus juice and dissolve the gelatin. Chill in refrigerator. Sieve asparagus (remove any tough ends). When gelatin is thick, add to mayonnaise. Stir in the lemon juice. Fold whipped cream into the mixture, then add sieved asparagus and seasonings (season highly).

Pour into mold that has been oiled with mayonnaise. Refrigerate until serving time. May be prepared 24 hours in advance. This is pretty served on California red lettuce leaves. Will serve a crowd when served with water crackers or crudites.

Sweet Potato Biscuits, Ham, and Chutney Butter

Smoked turkey may be substituted for the ham

Sweet Potato Biscuits (page
    67) cut into 2½-inch
    rounds
1 pound thin slices of ham
    (country ham or another
    good quality)
½ cup unsalted butter,
    softened

4 scallions, minced
¼ cup bottled mango chut-
    ney, minced
2 tablespoons Dijon-style
    mustard, or to taste
Flat leaf parsley for garnish,
    if desired

Assemble sweet potato biscuits and sliced ham. Make chutney butter: cream butter, scallions, chutney and mustard.

Split biscuits, spread with chutney butter and place sliced ham between the biscuit halves.

Sandwiches may be made one day ahead. Keep covered and chilled. Heat the sandwiches wrapped in foil in a 350° preheated oven 15–20 minutes, until heated through.

Garnish with parsley and serve.

Chocolate Orange Sauce with Fresh Fruit

A heavenly dip for fruit

3¼ cups sugar
⅔ cup (scant) cocoa
⅛ teaspoon salt
1½ cups light cream
¼ cup butter
1 teaspoon vanilla extract
1 to 1⅓ cups heavy cream
  (or desired consistency)

⅓ cup Grand Marnier (or to
  taste)
Fruits in season, cut into
  bite-size pieces
Pound cake or angel food
  cake

In a four-quart saucepan, stir together sugar, cocoa and salt. Add cream while stirring.   Cook over medium heat , stirring constantly until mixture comes to a full rolling boil. Boil without stirring to 234° or until syrup, when dropped in cold water, forms a ball.

Remove from heat and add butter and vanilla extract. Stir and cool to lukewarm. Add cream and Grand Marnier for desired consistency and taste.

To serve: Reheat and place in a chafing dish or fondue pot. Serve with fruits in season and pieces of pound cake or angel food cake.

Cranberry Pecan Tassies

Festive with a great flavor

1 (3-ounce) package cream
  cheese, softened
½ cup butter or margarine,
  softened
1 cup all-purpose flour
1 egg
¾ cup brown sugar, packed

1 teaspoon vanilla
⅛ teaspoon salt
⅓ cup fresh cranberries,
  finely chopped
3 tablespoons pecans,
  chopped

Combine cream cheese and butter. Stir in flour. Cover and chill one hour. Shape into 24 balls. Place in mini-muffin tins. Press dough against bottom and sides of cups. Beat together egg, brown sugar, vanilla and salt until smooth. Stir in cranberries and pecans. Spoon into pastry shells. Bake in a preheated 325° oven 30–35 minutes or until pastry is golden brown. Cool in pans. Run a knife around the edge to remove. Makes 24 tassies.

It's a New Year's Eve Party—
New Orleans Style

Katherine's Shrimp Creole Risotto
Roast Fresh Ham—Cajun Style
Onli's Crab Cakes with
   Cilantro Lime Mayonnaise
Oyster and Artichoke Dip with
      Fresh Whole Artichokes
Thurman's New Potatoes
Black-Eyed Pea Salad
Pasta Paté
Praline Cheesecake
Praline Lace Cookies

Katherine's Shrimp Creole Risotto

A simple and superb recipe

¼ cup salad oil
1 cup onion, chopped
½ cup green pepper,
  chopped
1½ cups rice, uncooked and
  washed
1 (6-ounce) can tomato paste

2½ cups chicken stock
  (you may use canned or
  bouillon)
1½ teaspoons salt
1½ teaspoons pepper
½ teaspoon thyme
2 cups shrimp, cooked

Heat oil in a heavy pan with a tight fitting lid. Fry onions and green peppers until tender, but not brown. Add rice, stir until slightly tan. Mix the remaining ingredients, except shrimp. Stir into the rice mixture. Cover tightly and simmer without removing the lid for 30 minutes. Stir in shrimp. Cook on low, stirring, for 10 minutes. Serve in a chafing dish.

Roast Fresh Ham—Cajun Style

Enjoy!

14 to 16-pound fresh ham
3 tablespoons coarse salt
1 tablespoon dried thyme
2 teaspoons pepper
2 cups plus 2 tablespoons cider vinegar, divided
1 cup dry white wine

1 tablespoon arrowroot
Small hard rolls
Hot Honey-Mustard (page 104)
Pepper Jelly
Mayonnaise

Ask the butcher to remove the aitchbone from the ham. Remove rind leaving ⅓-inch fat. Score fat in diamond pattern. Rub with salt, thyme, and pepper. Cover with plastic wrap and place in refrigerator overnight. Bring to room temperature and wipe dry. Place it, fat side up, on a rack in a roasting pan. Pour ½ cups vinegar over ham. Sear it in a preheated 425° oven 25 minutes. Reduce heat to 325°. Baste frequently with pan juice for 2 hours and 30 minutes. Remove ham. Skim fat from pan juice and deglaze with wine, reducing by half. Add 1 cup water and ½ cup vinegar. Reduce liquid to about 1½ cups.

Pour pan juice into a bowl and return ham to roasting pan. Baste and roast 1½–2 hours more, basting every 15 minutes. Meat thermometer should register 167° when done. Let ham rest for at least 15 minutes before slicing.

To make gravy: Mix arrowroot with 2 tablespoons cold water. Skim fat from pan juice. Add 3 cups water. Deglaze the pan, scraping up brown bits. Reduce to 2 cups. Strain into a small saucepan. Bring to a boil and stir in arrowroot mixture, whisking. Simmer sauce for 2 minutes, or until slightly thickened. Add any juice from the standing roast and 1–2 tablespoons of the vinegar, to taste. Transfer sauce to a sauce boat.

Serve ham with small hard rolls and gravy, plus separate bowls of hot honey mustard, pepper jelly, and mayonnaise.

Open-face sandwiches should have a colorful garnish keyed to the spread used. Cut bread into desired shapes with a cookie cutter and try olive on cheese spread, parsley on avocado, watercress on deviled ham, pimento strips on cream cheese and pickle slices on cheese.

Onli's Crab Cakes
Serve with Cilantro Lime Mayonnaise

1 pound white lump crabmeat or 2 cans white lump crabmeat
2 red peppers, chopped into ¼-inch pieces
1 green pepper, chopped into ¼-inch pieces
1 yellow pepper, chopped into ¼-inch pieces
1 medium yellow onion, chopped into ¼-inch pieces
3 green onions, chopped
1 teaspoon garlic, chopped
1 small can water chestnuts, chopped and drained
2 cups cracker crumbs
½ cup fresh lemon juice (use to taste)
1 package dry herbed bread dressing
½ of an 8x8-inch pan of cornbread, crumbled
4 eggs, well beaten
½ pound butter (no substitutions), melted (you may need more)
¼ teaspoon five spice powder
Pinch of nutmeg
½ teaspoon basil
½ teaspoon tarragon
Creole or Greek Seasoning, optional
Tabasco sauce, to taste
3 or 4 eggs, beaten
2–3 cups cracker crumbs

Mix together chopped ingredients, dry crumbs (cracker, herbed dressing, cornbread), melted butter, lemon juice, eggs, and crab. Add spices and taste as you go. Add crab last to preserve some of the lump shape in the cake. Form mixture into cakes with your hands.

Place beaten eggs in a pie plate and cracker crumbs in another pie plate. Dip cake in egg, then roll in cracker crumbs. Deep oil fry until light golden brown.

These cakes can be made and frozen before frying and remain fresh for up to 4 weeks. Makes 30 appetizers or 15 entrées.

Cilantro Lime Mayonnaise
Great with seafood

½ cup mayonnaise (you may use the light)
2 tablespoons cilantro, finely chopped
1 teaspoon lime peel, shredded
2 tablespoons fresh lime juice

Mix together, cover and chill. Makes 1 cup.

Oyster and Artichoke Dip

Serve with artichoke leaves as dippers

2 dozen oysters with their
water
1 (14-ounce) can artichoke
hearts, with water
2 bunches green onions,
chopped
½ pound butter

5 tablespoons flour
2 bay leaves
Salt to taste
White pepper to taste
5 or 6 whole fresh arti-
chokes

Poach oysters in their own water until their edges slightly curl. Strain water and mix with the artichoke water. Roughly chop oysters and artichoke hearts (you want a little texture).

Chop onions and sauté in melted butter until transparent. Add flour. Cook, stirring constantly, for 5 minutes. Slowly stir in oyster water mixture until you reach the desired consistency (it should be a little thick). Add bay leaves, salt and pepper.

Slowly bring to a boil. Add oysters and artichokes. Add more of the water if needed and cook, stirring for a few more minutes. Remove bay leaves. Serve from a chafing dish with whole artichokes around it. Guest pull off leaves and use for dippers.

If desired, you may use fresh artichoke bottoms and their water instead of canned and serve with leaves around the chafing dish. Will serve 35–45 people.

Fresh Whole Artichokes

A New Orleans favorite

5–6 artichokes, depending
on size
1 rib celery
1 onion, quartered

1 clove garlic
1 lemon, halved
1 tablespoon salt
1 teaspoon black pepper

Remove tough stems and bottom leaves from the artichokes. Stand upright in a large pot and cover with cold water. Soak for 1 hour. Add all the above ingredients, squeezing lemon as you add it. Cover pot and bring to a boil. Simmer 25–45 minutes, depending upon size, or until an outer leaf is easily removed. Drain well.

Thurman's New Potatoes
with Creme Fraiche and Caviar
A classic combination of tastes

**12 small new potatoes,
as much alike in size as
possible
½ cup Creme Fraiche or sour
cream**

**2 (2-ounce) jars caviar
Chives for garnish**

Cut each tiny potato in half crosswise, as uniformly in size as possible. Cut a thin slice off the skin end of each potato half to form a flat base. With a small scoop or spoon, scoop out center of each potato, leaving a shell about ¼-inch thick on bottom and sides.

Cover potatoes in water in a large kettle and bring to a boil. Reduce heat and boil gently 4–6 minutes until tender (not mushy). Drain well. Cool. Pat dry on paper towels.

Arrange potatoes, hollow side up, on serving plate. Cover and refrigerate until cold.

To serve: Fill center of potato with Creme Fraiche. Garnish with caviar and a chive stick. Makes 24.

Black-Eyed Pea Salad
Serve with endive leaves as scoops

**1½ pounds (3½ cups) dried
black-eyed peas
2 teaspoons salt
⅔ cup white wine vinegar
¾ cup olive oil
1 cup red onion, minced**

**½ cup tiny marinated cock-
tail onions (commercial),
or
½ cup green onions,
minced
1 cup bell pepper, minced
½ cup fresh parsley, minced
6 heads of endive**

Pick over and rinse black-eyed peas. Soak over night in 3 inches of water to cover. Bring to a boil, simmer, skimming froth. Add salt the last 5–10 minutes. Cook until tender. Drain and rinse. Blend vinegar and oil. Add to peas while they are warm. Add red onion, cocktail onions (with a little of their juice, to taste), green onion, bell pepper and fresh parsley. Make a day ahead and refrigerate.

Remove the bottoms of the heads of endive. Rinse and dry the leaves. Chill. Serve on a large platter around the bowl of peas that has been brought to room temperature. Makes 11 or 12 cups.

Pasta Paté

An imaginative appetizer by Bobbie Jean Sanders

5 ounces egg noodles or fettuccini, cooked and drained

2 (8-ounces) packages small elbow macaroni

2 (8-ounce) packages cream cheese

8 ounces cheddar or Mozzarella cheese, grated

8 ounces sour cream or more for consistency

3 tablespoons red onion, minced

½ cup sweet red pepper, finely chopped

½ cup green bell pepper, finely chopped

½ cup yellow pepper, finely chopped

½ cup parsley, finely chopped

½ teaspoon cayenne pepper

1 teaspoon Greek or Cajun seasoning

Salt to taste

½ cup Parmesan cheese, grated

Cook pasta and drain well. Should equal about 1 pound pasta cooked.

In a large bowl, combine cream cheese, cheddar cheese, sour cream, onion, peppers, and parsley. Stir in seasonings to taste. Gently fold mixture into pasta.

Lightly oil a bread loaf pan. Sprinkle Parmesan cheese over the bottom. Pour pasta into pan and pack down. Cover with plastic wrap, then several layers of foil. Place something heavy on top (canned goods will do) to pack while chilling in the refrigerator overnight.

Unmold the paté and garnish with long stems of chives and small tomato roses, or red, yellow and green pepper rings. Serve with Danish black or dark rye bread cut into small rounds. Guests slice a bit of paté to spread on bread rounds.

To serve as a first course, dip a slice of tomato in olive oil and sprinkle with basil. Place on a bread round. Serve with a slice of paté and a few asparagus spears that have been dipped into Italian dressing and chilled.

Praline Cheesecake

Serve with Pecan Praline Cookies

2 cups honey graham
cracker crumbs
2 tablespoons sugar
6 tablespoons butter, melted
3 (8-ounce) packages cream
cheese, softened
4 eggs
2 cups dark brown sugar,
packed

1½ teaspoon instant coffee
1 tablespoon vanilla
⅛ teaspoon salt
½ cup pecans, chopped
12–15 pecan halves for
garnish
Butter

Blend graham cracker crumbs with sugar and butter. Press into the bottom and sides of a buttered springform pan. Preheat oven to 350°.

Mix the cream cheese with eggs and sugar, adding eggs one at a time and beating well after each addition. Add instant coffee, vanilla, salt, and pecans. Mix until well blended. Pour into prepared pan and bake 40–45 minutes. Cool to room temperature, then chill.

To serve, top with pecan halves that have been toasted and lightly tossed in melted butter. Serve with Praline Lace Cookies.

Praline Lace Cookies

A Creole delicacy made with pecans

1½ cups pecans, chopped
1 cup sugar
4 tablespoons flour
⅓ teaspoon baking powder

⅛ teaspoon salt
½ cup butter, melted
2 teaspoons vanilla
1 egg, beaten

Mix well the pecans, sugar, flour, baking powder and salt. Add melted butter, vanilla and egg. Cover and refrigerate overnight. Drop onto foil lined cookie sheet by teaspoonfuls. Place about 3 inches apart. Bake in a 325° oven for 10–12 minutes. Let cool and peel off the foil. Makes about 4 dozen.

EVERYBODY LOVES THE COCKTAIL HOUR

Come Meet Our New Neighbors

Come for Cocktails at 5 O'Clock

We Have an Engagement to
Announce

Come and Smell the Roses
in Our Garden

The Frost is on the Pumpkin—
Let's Party!

Opportunities to serve light cocktail foods are endless. Large receptions such as anniversary or engagement celebrations lend themselves well to this type party. They usually take place at an earlier hour, and the invitation often has a cut-off time, such as 5 until 7 p.m.

Having friends over for drinks before going to dinner at a restaurant is one of the most popular occasions for serving hors d'oeuvres. Any combination of two or three savories in this chapter will answer the question of what to offer with a glass of wine or a cocktail that will not spoil appetites for dinner.

We have dispensed with the first course chapter found in our original book because we feel there are few occasions for formal service with today's casual lifestyle. However, serving several light hors d'oeuvres on a salad plate before dinner fills this niche very nicely.

Come Meet Our New Neighbors

Sandra's Olive Cheese Balls
Squash Dip
Easie's Marinated Cheese
Courtney's Sesame-Parmesan Chicken
Oatmeal Crisps
Jalapeno, Crab and Artichoke Dip
Chocolate-Orange Sandwich Cookies

Sandra's Olive Cheese Balls

Tasty tidbits to pass around

2 cups sharp cheddar cheese, finely grated
½ cup butter, room temperature
1 cup flour, sifted

½ teaspoon salt
1 teaspoon paprika
¼ teaspoon Tabasco sauce
Olives stuffed with pimentos

Cream cheese and butter. Sift in flour and other dry ingredients. Add Tabasco. Break off pinches of dough and wrap around each olive. Place balls on cookie sheets and bake in pre-heated 400° oven for 15 minutes. May be frozen on cookie sheets, placed in baggies and taken out to bake as needed. Makes approximately 5 dozen.

 Serve your favorite cheese spreads in clean clay flower pots placed on a large clay saucer to hold crackers. Put a straw in the cheese spread and a flower in the straw. Sprinkle poppy seeds or chopped nuts on top of the spread.

Squash Dip

Hot and creamy. Can be made ahead, then baked at party time

**2 pounds yellow squash,
  boiled whole**
⅓ cup margarine
½ cup onions, chopped
**4 ounces cream cheese,
  softened**
**1 ¼ cups mild cheddar
  cheese, grated**

**⅓ cup Parmesan cheese,
  grated**
½ cup sour cream
¼ cup dry white wine
1 teaspoon salt
1 teaspoon sugar
½ teaspoon lemon pepper
1 egg, beaten

Drain squash well and slice in half lengthwise. Remove seeds with a teaspoon and purée in food processor until smooth. Chop squash coarsely with quick motions in processor. Stir into seed mixture. Melt margarine in a skillet and sauté onions until tender. Drain and stir into squash mixture.

Beat softened cream cheese in a mixer and blend in other cheeses. Mix in sour cream, wine, and seasonings. Add squash mixture and combine well. Blend in beaten egg. Bake at 350° in greased 2-quart casserole for 30 minutes or until set. Serve warm with chips or crackers.

Easie's Marinated Cheese

Looks elegant in a glass dish

½ cup olive oil
½ cup white wine vinegar
**1 (2-ounce) jar diced
  pimentos, drained**
**3 tablespoons fresh parsley,
  chopped**
**3 tablespoons green onions,
  minced**
3 cloves garlic, minced

1 teaspoon sugar
¾ teaspoon dried basil
½ teaspoon salt
**½ teaspoon freshly ground
  pepper**
**1 (8-ounce) block sharp
  cheddar cheese, chilled**
**1 (8-ounce) package cream
  cheese**

Combine first 10 ingredients in a jar. Cover and shake well.

Cut cheddar cheese and cream cheese in half lengthwise. Cut each half crosswise into ¼-inch thick slices. Arrange cheese slices alternately in a shallow dish, standing slices on edge. Pour marinade over cheese. Cover and refrigerate for 8 hours. Drain liquid and arrange slices on serving platter topped with the pimento, parsley and green onions. Serve with crackers.

Courtney's Sesame-Parmesan Chicken

Prepare ahead and freeze; fry before serving

½ cup Parmesan cheese, grated
½ cup sesame seeds
2 tablespoons dry fines herbs
2 eggs, beaten

1 cup flour
1 pound boneless, skinless chicken breasts, cut into strips
Salt and pepper to taste
2 quarts cooking oil

Combine Parmesan, sesame seeds and herbs in a bowl. Place another bowl containing the beaten eggs beside it. Place flour in a third bowl. Dip chicken strips, which should be 3 inches long and ½-inch thick, in the flour, then the egg, then the Parmesan mixture. Salt and pepper to taste. Shake off excess after dredging in each ingredient. Lay strips in a single layer on a tray lined with aluminum foil. Cover with plastic wrap and freeze. Once frozen, strips may be placed in a freezer bag and returned to freezer.

Immediately before serving, heat oil in a large pan to 375°. Cook a few pieces of chicken at a time while still frozen. Cool for 3–4 minutes. Serve with Mustard Sauce.

MUSTARD SAUCE

½ cup sour cream   ¼ cup grainy, country mustard

Combine ingredients well. Chill until needed.

Oatmeal Crisps

Comforting flavor of cinnamon and oatmeal

2 sticks margarine
2 sticks butter
2 cups sugar
1 egg
2 cups flour, sifted
1 teaspoon baking soda
¼ teaspoon salt

1 teaspoon baking soda
¼ teaspoon salt
1 teaspoon cinnamon
4 cups instant (1-minute) oatmeal
½ teaspoon vanilla extract
Confectioners' sugar

Cream margarine, butter, and sugar with electric mixer. Add remaining ingredients and mix well. Drop by teaspoonfuls onto ungreased baking sheet. Flatten with fork dipped in cold water. Bake 10–12 minutes in 350° oven. When done, cool slightly and sprinkle with confectioners' sugar. Makes 8 dozen.

Jalapeño, Crab, and Artichoke Dip
Guests can't resist this unusual Mexican dip

¾ cup green bell pepper,
  chopped
1 cup onion, chopped
3 tablespoons margarine,
  melted
2 cups light mayonnaise
2 (14-ounce) cans artichoke
  hearts, drained and
  chopped
⅓ cup cilantro, minced

1 cup Parmesan cheese,
  grated
1 tablespoon Worcestershire
  sauce
1 or 2 drops Tabasco sauce
2 canned jalapeño peppers,
  chopped
¼ teaspoon cumin
1 pound crab meat
1 cup cheddar cheese, grated

Sauté the green bell pepper and onion in melted margarine until translucent. Measure the light mayonnaise into a large bowl and stir in the green bell pepper mixture, chopped artichoke hearts, cilantro, Parmesan cheese, seasonings and sauces, jalapeño peppers, and crab which has been picked over well. Blend well. Spoon the mixture into a greased two quart baking dish. Sprinkle cheddar cheese over top. Bake in a 350° oven for 10 minutes, covered. Uncover and bake 20 more minutes. Serve hot with bagel crisps.

Chocolate-Orange Sandwich Cookies
An unusual flavor combination that is always a hit

1¼ cups butter
2 cups sugar
2 eggs
2 teaspoons vanilla

2 cups flour
¾ cup cocoa
1 teaspoon soda
½ teaspoon salt

Cream butter and sugar; add eggs and vanilla. Combine dry ingredients and stir in egg mixture. Drop by teaspoonfuls onto an ungreased cookie sheet. Bake at 350° for 8–10 minutes. Cool for about 2 minutes, then transfer to a wire rack. When thoroughly cool, spread Orange Filling on half of cookies; top with remaining halves to make 5 dozen sandwiches.

Orange Filling:

3 tablespoons butter
3 tablespoons heavy cream
1 cup powdered sugar, sifted

Grated rind of 1 medium
  orange
1 tablespoon Grand Marnier

Place butter and cream in a bowl; set over a pan of hot water; stir until butter melts. Remove from heat. Stir in remaining ingredients; beat until thick.

Come for Cocktails
at 5 O'Clock

Smoked Salmon Presentation with
Caper-Dill Sauce
Toast Points
Cocktail Carrots
Mexican Pinwheels
Frosted Lemon Tea Biscuits
Patti's Hot Sausage Dip
Chocolate Lime Tarts

Smoked Salmon Presentation

An elegant but easy way to serve the popular appetizer

**2–3 pounds ready-smoked
  salmon**
Fresh dill
Fresh fennel
**3 pepper halves (red,
  green, yellow)**

Lemon twists, thinly sliced
Green onions, chopped
Caper-Dill Sauce
Toast points

If salmon is unsliced, slice it against the grain on the diagonal. Place
it on a long, narrow dish and decorate it with sprigs of dill and
fennel. Cut peppers in half and scoop out inside fibers. Fill one
pepper half with lemon twists, another with chopped green onions,
and the remaining one with Caper-Dill Sauce. Place filled pepper
halves on platter beside salmon. Use teaspoon as server for onions,
cocktail fork for lemon twists and butter knife for sauce. Place toast
points in a basket, lined with a linen napkin.

Caper-Dill Sauce

This is also good as a dip for raw vegetables

½ cup sour cream
½ cup mayonnaise
2 tablespoons capers

1 tablespoon fresh dill, chopped (1 teaspoon dried)

Mix together, chill, serve in a pepper half.

Toast Points

Equally good with dips

White bread
Melted margarine

Lemon pepper

Trim crusts from bread. Slice diagonally. Brush with melted margarine mixed with lemon pepper. Bake 20 minutes at 250°. Change shelves. Bake 20 more minutes.

Cocktail Carrots

They keep two weeks in the fridge

1 pound miniature carrots, peeled
2 bay leaves
½ cup white wine vinegar
¼ cup water
3 tablespoons sugar

½ teaspoon salt
½ teaspoon dried mustard
1 teaspoon dill
½ teaspoon basil
1 clove garlic, minced
Chopped parsley

Cook carrots until barely tender. Drain and run cold water over them until cool. Mix remaining ingredients except parsley. Marinate carrots in mixture for at least 48 hours. Drain and serve garnished with parsley.

Mexican Pinwheels

Bite-sized stuffed tortillas

20 flour tortillas
2 (8-ounce) packages cream cheese
²/₃ cup sour cream
½ cup green onions, chopped
2 tablespoons green onion tops, chopped

¼ cup red pepper, chopped
2 canned jalapeno peppers, chopped
2 teaspoons picante sauce
2 teaspoons lime juice
½ teaspoon garlic salt
¼ teaspoon cumin
2 teaspoons Worcestershire sauce

Bring tortillas to room temperature. Combine cream cheese and sour cream in a mixer. Blend in remaining ingredients. Spread cream cheese mixture on tortillas. Roll up tortillas and refrigerate overnight. Trim ends and cut tortillas into one-inch slices. Serve at once or return them to the refrigerator where they may remain for up to two hours. Makes approximately 120 bite-sized servings.

Frosted Lemon Tea Biscuits

Old-fashioned tea cakes with a lemon tang

4 cups flour
1 cup sugar
3 teaspoons baking powder
1 cup shortening

1 teaspoon lemon extract
1 egg, beaten, plus enough milk to make 1 cup

Preheat oven to 375°. Mix flour, sugar and baking powder in a large bowl. Cut in shortening with a pastry blender, or combine at low speed in a mixer until consistency of meal. Add lemon extract to egg and milk mixture. Add all to dry ingredients. Mix well and turn onto a floured board. Roll to ¼-inch thickness and cut into rounds with a biscuit cutter. Place on lightly greased cookie sheet and bake 15–20 minutes. Cool on racks. Makes approximately 6 dozen. The biscuits will be semisweet, but the frosting will make them sweeter.

LEMON FROSTING:

2½ cups confectioners' sugar, sifted
½ cup unsalted butter, melted

2 tablespoons lemon juice
1 tablespoon lemon rind, grated

Combine ingredients and use them to frost lemon biscuits.

Patti's Hot Sausage Dip

Warm and filling on a cool day

1 pound hot sausage
1 (8-ounce) package cream cheese (low fat, optional)
1 (8-ounce) carton sour cream
8-ounces cheddar cheese, grated

1 (4-ounce) can chopped green chilies
1 loaf French or Hawaiian bread

Brown sausage and drain. Blend cream cheese, sour cream and sausage in mixer. Add cheddar cheese and chili peppers and stir in by hand. Hollow out 1 long, thick loaf of French bread or 1 round of Hawaiian bread with a spoon and fill center with dip. Wrap in heavy duty foil and bake for 1 hour at 350°. Serve with corn chips or pull off portions of bread.

Chocolate Lime Tarts

Two distinct tastes that combine well

3 egg yolks
1 (14-ounce) can sweetened condensed milk
4 ounces unsweetened chocolate, melted

⅓ cup lime juice
Cream Cheese Pastry
Kiwi fruit, sour cream

Beat egg yolks at high speed for 4 minutes. Add condensed milk, melted chocolate and lime juice. Beat well.

Spoon filling into pastry lined mini-muffin tins. Bake at 400° for 15–18 minutes. Cool. Remove from tins. Garnish with kiwi fruit slices cut into fourths. Top with a dab of sour cream. Makes 3½ dozen tarts.

CREAM CHEESE PASTRY:

1 cup butter or margarine, room temperature
6 ounces cream cheese, room temperature

2 cups flour, sifted

Cream butter and cream cheese together until smooth. Add flour, mixing well. Shape dough into a ball; chill 8 hours. Break off marble-sized pieces of dough and press into greased 1-inch muffin tins.

We Have an Engagement to Announce

Down-South Caviar with Crostini
Carlene Scanlon's Shrimp Vegetable
Medley Vinaigrette
Pepperoni Pizza Dip
Roasted Red Pepper and Goat Cheese Dip
Sue's Marinated Mushrooms
Jan's Petite Pavlovas
Nikki's Double-Frosted Bourbon Brownies

Down-South Caviar
So easy it almost makes itself

**1 (11-ounce) can white
shoepeg corn, drained
2 (15-ounce) cans black-eyed
peas, drained
1 cup medium or hot salsa**

**1 medium onion, chopped
1 medium green pepper,
chopped
2 tablespoons fresh cilantro,
chopped**

Combine all ingredients and stir well. Refrigerate 24 hours. Serve with Crostini.

Crostini
May be made a week ahead

**2 thin loaves French bread
(baguettes)**   **1 cup extra-virgin olive oil**

Preheat oven to 350°. Slice bread in ¼-inch slices and arrange slices on baking sheets. Brush with olive oil. Bake for 8–10 minutes until lightly browned. Store in tins. Before serving, may be re-crisped in 300° oven. Yield: 6½ dozen.

Carlene Scanlon's Shrimp Vegetable Medley Vinaigrette

To use as a salad, spoon onto lettuce leaves

10 pounds shrimp
2 boxes crab boil mixture
Lemon juice
2 (6-ounce) jars whole
mushrooms, drained
1 (14-ounce) can hearts of
palm, drained and sliced

1 (14-ounce) can artichoke
hearts, drained and
quartered
1 (8-ounce) can water chest-
nuts, drained and sliced
Romaine lettuce leaves

Boil shrimp for 3 minutes in water seasoned with crab boil mixture; drain, peel and devein. Refrigerate shrimp in a bowl covered with plastic wrap. Chill thoroughly. Pour dressing over shrimp and sprinkle with lemon juice. Toss lightly and refrigerate overnight. Add all ingredients except romaine and continue to marinate for 24 hours, stirring every 12 hours. Pour salad into a crystal bowl lined with romaine lettuce leaves. Place in a larger bowl of ice. Serve with toothpicks.

VINAIGRETTE DRESSING:

2¼ cups olive oil
¾ cup white wine vinegar
1 tablespoon Dijon mustard
2½ teaspoons salt

Freshly ground pepper to
taste
1½ teaspoons dill weed

Combine all ingredients and mix well.

Pepperoni Pizza Dip

Warms your bones on a winter day

1 (8-ounce) package cream cheese, softened
½ cup sour cream
1 teaspoon dried oregano, crushed
⅛ teaspoon garlic powder
⅛ teaspoon red pepper (optional)
½ cup pizza sauce

½ cup pepperoni, chopped
¼ cup green onions, sliced
¼ cup green peppers, chopped
½ cup mozzarella cheese, shredded
1 small can ripe olives, sliced

Beat first 5 ingredients together and spread evenly in a 9 or 10-inch quiche dish or pie plate. Spread pizza sauce over the top; sprinkle with pepperoni, green onions and green pepper. Bake at 350° for 10 minutes. Top with cheese and olives and bake 5 minutes or until cheese is melted and mixture is heated. Makes 1½ cups. Serve with crackers.

Roasted Red Pepper and Goat Cheese Dip

Serve with fresh vegetable dippers or bagel chips

2 red peppers, roasted and chopped
3 cloves garlic, roasted and chopped
1½ cups mild goat cheese, crumbled
1½ tablespoons olive oil
1 teaspoon fresh thyme, chopped

¼ cup fresh basil, chopped
1 tablespoon fresh rosemary, chopped
3 green onions, chopped
Seasoning salt and pepper to taste

Place red peppers, garlic and goat cheese in food processor and purée until smooth. Add seasonings and mix in. Refrigerate until serving time. Makes 1½ cups.

 Goat cheese is, by extension, goats' milk cheese that is soft and fresh, uncooked and unprocessed. It is also called chèvre.

Sue's Marinated Mushrooms

Can also be served as a side dish

¾ cup salad oil
3 tablespoons soy sauce
⅛ cup Worcestershire sauce
1 teaspoon salt
3 tablespoons lemon juice

¼ teaspoon garlic powder
1 teaspoon pepper
⅓ cup red wine
1½–2 pounds fresh mushrooms

Mix all ingredients except mushrooms in large saucepan. Place mushrooms, stem up, in pan. Cook on medium heat 15 minutes. Turn mushrooms and cook 10 minutes more. Reheat before serving. Flavor improves if done two days in advance. Serve with toothpicks.

Jan's Petite Pavlovas

Light as a cloud, they melt in your mouth

MERINGUES:

6 egg whites
½ teaspoon cream of tartar
¼ teaspoon salt

1½ teaspoons vanilla
1½ cups sugar

Have egg whites at room temperature. Add cream of tartar, salt and vanilla. Beat until frothy. Gradually add sugar, a small amount at a time, beating until very stiff peaks form and sugar is dissolved.

Cover cookie sheets with plain ungreased paper (grocery sacks do fine). Use a teaspoon to drip mixture into 2–2½ inch circles. Scoop indentation in centers with bowl of spoon.

Bake for 1 hour at 250°. Turn oven off but do not open door. Leave in oven at least two hours or overnight.

FILLING:

1 (8-ounce) package cream cheese, softened
1 cup sugar
1 cup heavy cream, whipped

1 teaspoon vanilla
1 teaspoon almond extract
Kiwi fruit

Cream the cream cheese and sugar. Fold in whipped cream. Add vanilla and almond extract. Fill meringue shells and top with slice of Kiwi fruit (or ½ slice). Makes 7 dozen.

The filling cannot be added until shortly before serving or meringue will become soggy. Also, filled meringues cannot be refrigerated.

Nikki's Double-Frosted
Bourbon Brownies

The chocoholics on your list will think they're in heaven!

¼ cup butter
2 squares unsweetened
 chocolate
2 eggs
1 cup sugar
½ cup flour
¼ teaspoon salt

1 teaspoon vanilla
6 ounces semisweet choco-
 late chips
4 tablespoons bourbon,
 optional

Melt butter and chocolate in a double boiler over low heat. Beat eggs until light. Beat in sugar until thick. Add chocolate mixture, flour and salt. Mix. Stir in vanilla and chocolate chips. Pour into a buttered 8 or 9-inch square pan. Bake at 375° for 15–20 minutes. Remove from oven, punch holes in the brownies with a fork and pour in bourbon while hot. Cool.

FROSTING:

½ cup butter, room temperature

2 cups powdered sugar,
 sifted
1 teaspoon vanilla

Cream butter and sugar. Mix in vanilla. Chill ½ hour to solidify. Frost brownies.

GLAZE:

1 square unsweetened
 chocolate

1 tablespoon butter

Melt butter and chocolate. Cool. Drizzle over white frosting layer. Brownies may be frozen. Makes 3 dozen.

Come and Smell the Roses in Our Garden

Mosaic Chicken and Vegetable Terrine
Roasted Asparagus with Bagna Caude
Tomato Tapenade in Squash Cups
Butchie Nation's Tuna Paté
Rosanna Hickman's Elegant Stuffed Brie
Emily's Pimento Cheese Triangles
Watermelon Ambrosia
Beth's Bird Nest Macaroons
Strawberry Profitteroles

Mosaic Chicken and Vegetable Terrine

Jo's most requested recipe

4 long carrots, quartered lengthwise (about 8 ounces)
10 ounces fresh or frozen green peas
1 large ripe avocado
Juice of ½ lemon
Salt
Fresh ground pepper
1 pound boned chicken breast, trimmed of fat
1½ cups chicken broth (canned may be used)
6 tablespoons fresh lemon juice

2 tablespoons fresh tarragon, chopped, or 1 teaspoon dried
2 tablespoons Dijon mustard
4 tablespoons butter, chilled
3 egg whites, chilled
1 cup vegetable oil
14–16 bottled or canned grape leaves
2 cucumbers, sliced
2 zucchini squash, sliced
2 carrots, sliced in rounds
8 celery ribs, cut in 1½-inch pieces
Water crackers

Cook the cut carrots in boiling salted water until tender enough to cut easily, but not mushy. Drain and refresh with cold water. Cook peas about 1 minute. Drain and refresh in cold water. Pat dry. Halve avocado lengthwise, peel and slice ½-inch thick. Coat with juice of ½ lemon. Season all vegetables with salt and pepper and refrigerate.

Continued

Simmer chicken about 8 minutes in chicken broth or until tender. Remove, let cool and cut into small cubes. Add 6 tablespoons lemon juice, salt and pepper. Chill one hour.

Chill food processor container and purée chicken in it. Add tarragon, mustard and butter, cut into small pieces. Process 3 or 4 seconds. Add chilled egg whites and blend. Add oil a little at a time with processor running. Refrigerate mixture until ready to assemble.

To assemble: Rinse grape leaves in cool water several times and pat dry. Lightly oil a small long terrine. (If you wish to use a bread loaf pan for a large party, make the vegetables once and the chicken mixture twice. You will use about the same amount of grape leaves.) Spread grape leaves on bottom and sides with enough overhang to enclose terrine.

Spread ¼-inch thick layer of chicken mousse on leaves. Arrange avocado on mousse in one solid layer. Add more mousse and top with carrots, side by side in one layer. Add more filling, then green peas then remaining mousse. Fold over grape leaves and cover terrine with a piece of buttered brown paper.

Place terrine in a large pan and fill with hot water. It should come halfway up side of terrine. Bake 30 minutes in a 350° oven. Cool terrine in a pan of cool water. Refrigerate overnight. It is best made 2 or 3 days before serving.

To serve, place on a platter still in the grape leaves. Remove just enough leaves on one end for guest to start to slice and spread on water crackers. You may garnish with cucumber, squash and carrot slices and pieces of celery for spreading.

Roasted Asparagus with Bagna Caude
Make asparagus a day ahead

2 pounds asparagus
1 tablespoon extra-virgin
   olive oil
½ teaspoon salt

⅛ teaspoon black pepper,
   freshly grated
2 lemons

Preheat oven to 425°. Place asparagus, with wooded ends broken off and discarded, on a jellyroll pan or cookie sheet. Drizzle with oil and sprinkle with salt and pepper. Turn until evenly coated. Arrange in a single layer.

Roast 10–15 minutes, or until just tender and tips start to brown. Cool in pans, cover and refrigerate.

To serve: Reheat in 350° oven for 5 minutes. Cut lemon into wedges for garnish.

Bagna Cauda
This is also a wonderful hot dip with any crisp raw vegetable

1 cup butter or margarine
½ cup olive oil
5 large cloves garlic, minced
   or pressed
2 tablespoons lemon juice

1½ teaspoons ground black
   pepper
2 (2-ounce) cans flat an-
   chovy fillets, finely

Combine butter, oil, garlic, lemon juice, and pepper in a heat proof or chafing dish. Heat, stirring until butter melts. Drain anchovy oil into mixture. Add chopped anchovies and stir.

To serve: Keep sauce warm over a candle or low alcohol flame, or reheat periodically. Sauce may brown slightly but don't let it burn. Dip asparagus into sauce; hold a slice of bread under each bite to catch any drips as you eat. Makes 2 cups.

Serve cheese at room temperature. Remove from refrigerator 2 hours before serving. Roquefort should be served chilled. Keep covered with a damp cheesecloth until serving time.

Tomato Tapenade in Squash Cups

A perfect marriage of flavors

1 tablespoon olive oil
½ cup sweet red pepper, finely chopped
1 small red onion, finely chopped
2 large (1 pound) tomatoes, skinned, seeded, finely chopped
1 clove garlic, finely chopped
1 tablespoon lemon juice
1 tablespoon white wine or water

2 teaspoons fresh oregano, chopped, or ½ teaspoon dried
½ teaspoon sugar
¼ teaspoon salt
¼ teaspoon fresh black pepper
6–8 fresh-cured ripe olives, pitted and chopped
Squash cups
24 toasted pine nuts (optional)

Make the day before serving. Heat oil and cook pepper and onion until golden. Add all other ingredients except olives; cook, covered, stirring often until vegetables are soft and most of the liquid has evaporated. Stir in olives and cool. Cover and refrigerate.

Several hours, or the day before serving, place one teaspoon tapenade in each squash cup.

SQUASH CUPS:

½ pound zucchini (1½ inches in diameter)

½ pound yellow squash (1½ inches in diameter)

Prepare the day before serving. Cut squash into twenty-four, ¾-inch slices. Scoop out pulp and seeds, creating a ½-inch deep cup. Cook squash 1½ minutes in 3 inches of boiling water to cover. Drain and rinse with cold water. Pat dry. Place on serving dish; cover and refrigerate.

If desired, you may garnish with a toasted pine nut on top of each cup. Makes 24.

Butchie Nation's Tuna Paté

Fresh grilled tuna may be used instead of canned

1 (8-ounce) package cream
  cheese, softened
1 (6-ounce) can solid white
  albacore tuna, packed in
  water, drained

1 small onion, grated
¼ teaspoon Tabasco sauce
½ cup pecans (optional)
Salt and pepper to taste
½ cup fresh parsley,
  chopped

Blend cream cheese, tuna, onion, Tabasco, pecans, salt, pepper and 2 tablespoons parsley in food processor. Form in a roll or place in a crock. Roll in remaining parsley or sprinkle parsley on top of crock. Serve with crackers.

Note: Recipe may be doubled or tripled and made in any shape desired. Sprinkle heavily with parsley.

Rosanna Hickman's
Elegant Stuffed Brie

You may substitute camembert for this beautiful presentation

1 (8-ounce) wheel Brie or
  Camembert cheese
3 ounces cream cheese
2 ounces plain unsweetened
  yogurt or sherry
12 green seedless grapes,
  sliced in thirds

Whole grapes and grape
  halves for garnish
Watercress
Paprika

With a sharp knife cut the cheese wheel in half, sandwich fashion, to form a top and bottom.

Mix cream cheese with yogurt or sherry until smooth and slightly fluffy. Slice grapes into 3 pieces and gently stir them into the cheese mixture. Spread ⅔ on the bottom half of cheese. Place top of cheese on yogurt and dollop the other ⅓ of mixture on top.

Garnish top with grape halves and place whole green grapes and watercress decoratively around the base. Refrigerate.

Make the day you plan to serve. The grapes will darken the mixture. Remove from refrigerator 30 minutes before serving. Sprinkle on paprika. Serve with unseasoned crackers.

Emily's Pimento Cheese Triangles

The very best flavor

3 ounces cream cheese, softened
4 tablespoons mayonnaise
3 garlic cloves, minced
¼ cup fresh parsley, chopped
½ teaspoon Pickapepper sauce, or to taste
⅛ teaspoon hot sauce, or to taste
¾ cup pecans, coarsely chopped

1 (2-ounce) jar diced pimento and juice
12 ounces extra sharp cheddar cheese, grated
Alfalfa seed sprouts, if desired
1 loaf thin sliced whole wheat sandwich bread, crust removed

Purée the first 6 ingredients in a processor until smooth. Place in a bowl and add pecans, pimentos with juice, and grated cheddar cheese. Mix well. Refrigerate two hours or overnight.

Trim crust from bread. Spread half the loaf with cheese mixture. Top with a few sprouts, if desired and the other slices of bread. Cut into triangles. Makes 2½ cups cheese.

Watermelon Ambrosia

Serve in your prettiest glass bowl

1 watermelon, scooped into balls (6 cups)
2 pineapples, cut onto 1-inch cubes (6 cups) (pineapple in natural juice may be substituted)

1 cup sweetened, flaked coconut, lightly packed
¾ cup dark rum, or to taste

Cut and drain fruit. Place fruit in serving bowl or watermelon shell. Sprinkle coconut and rum over mixture and toss well. Chill covered at least 2 hours or overnight. Serve with picks or on plates. Serves approximately 25 people.

Beth's Bird Nest Macaroons
Colorful for spring or delicious served plain

COOKIES:

2½ cups Angel Flake
   coconut
⅔ cup sugar
¼ cup all-purpose flour
¼ teaspoon salt

4 egg whites
1 teaspoon almond extract
1 cup natural almonds,
   chopped

Combine coconut, granulated sugar, flour and salt. Stir in egg whites, almond extract and chopped almonds. Mix well.

Drop from a teaspoon, 2 inches apart, onto a lightly greased baking sheet. Make an indention in the center of each with finger. Preheat oven to 325°.

TOPPING:

1 roll of almond paste
¼ cup confectioners' sugar,
   or to taste

Food color in 4 pastel colors

Knead almond paste and confectioners' sugar together to taste. Divide evenly into 4 small bowls. Add 1–2 drops of food color to paste, making four different pastel shades. Knead until color is distributed evenly. Place a small amount of paste in each indention. Bake 20–25 minutes or until edges of cookies are golden brown. Makes 2½ dozen.

For a delicious plain macaroon, leave off the topping and do not indent tops.

Strawberry Profitteroles
Miniature cream puffs are easy to make

CREAM PUFFS:

1 cup water
½ cup butter or margarine
1 teaspoon sugar

¼ teaspoon salt
1 cup all-purpose flour,
  sifted
4 eggs

Bring water, butter, sugar and salt to a full rolling boil in a large saucepan. Add flour all at once. Stir vigorously with wooden spoon until mixture forms a thick smooth ball that leaves the sides of pan clean. Remove from heat and cool slightly.

Add eggs, one at a time, beating well after each until paste is shiny smooth. Shape a rounded teaspoon into a mound for each on cookie sheet 2 inches apart. Bake in preheated 400° oven 25 minutes or until crisp and golden. Remove from sheet and cool on wire rack. Makes 36 small puffs.

STRAWBERRY FILLING:

1 pint strawberries, washed,
  hulled and chopped
4 tablespoons granulated
  sugar

1 cup heavy cream, whipped
½ teaspoon almond extract
Confectioners' sugar

Stir 3 tablespoons sugar into prepared berries. Chill at least 30 minutes. Beat cream with remaining sugar and almond extract until stiff. Chill.

To serve, cut a slice from top of puffs. Remove any soft dough. Fold strawberries into cream. Fill puffs and replace tops. Sift confectioners' sugar over tops. Garnish with mint leaves and whole strawberries.

Flowers make beautiful garnishes for hors d'oeuvres or salads: Be sure they are edible and pesticide free. Remove stamens and styles from flower's center. A few common flowers that may be eaten are bachelor's buttons, carnations, violets, rose petals, scented geraniums, pansies, honeysuckle, daisies, dianthus, forget-me-nots, gardenias, marigolds, lilies, nasturtiums, impatiens. Wash flowers gently in room temperature water.

The Frost is on the Pumpkin—Let's Party!

Bobbie J's Boula Boula Soup
Chan Patterson's Sausage in
   Turban Squash
Emily's Autumn Fruit Composition
Louise Henshaw's Hot Asparagus
   Triangles
Emily Moore's Toasted Pecans
Almond Cheesecake

Bobbie J's Boula Boula Soup

An old Natchez Post House recipe

**1 (10-ounce) can green pea
   soup**
**1 (10-ounce) can green turtle
   soup**
2½ cups heavy cream
¼ cup dry sherry

⅛ teaspoon cayenne pepper
⅛ teaspoon salt, or to taste
2–3 drops Tabasco to taste
Light cream to thin soup
**½ pound crabmeat, finely
   chopped**

Heat soups together gently. Do not boil. Stir to blend. Add cream, sherry and seasonings. Thin to desired consistency with cream. Add picked over crabmeat carefully. Stir and serve. Serves approximately 24 in demitasse cups.

Chan Patterson's Sausage in Turban Squash

A pumpkin may be substituted for the squash

1 (3-pound) turban squash
1 pound bulk sausage
1 cup celery, chopped
¼ cup onion, chopped
½ cup fresh mushrooms,
  sliced
1 egg, slightly beaten

½ cup sour cream
¼ cup Parmesan cheese,
  grated
¼ teaspoon salt
*4 whole loaves bread,
  unsliced

Remove top of squash. Cut out seeds and sprinkle inside with salt. Place cut side down in a baking dish. Add 1 inch of water and bake in preheated 375° oven for 1 hour or until tender. Remove squash from pan; reserve water.

Cook sausage, celery and onion 5 minutes. Stir in mushrooms. Cook until meat is browned. Drain. Combine egg, sour cream, cheese and salt. Add to sausage mixture. Spoon into cavity of squash. Place in pan of water. Bake 20–25 minutes.

*Serve with several different shaped homemade bread loaves for guests to cut. It is a beautiful presentation when other fall vegetables are added for garnish.

Emily's Autumn Fruit Composition

Beautiful and easy

1 cantaloupe, peeled and
  seeded
1 pound seedless red grapes,
  washed

2 (8-ounce) cans pineapple
  chunks in natural juices

Cut cantaloupe into 1-inch cubes. Toss with green grapes. Add pineapple with its juice and stir to moisten all fruit. Cover and refrigerate 12 hours. To serve, drain away juice and place fruit in a pretty glass bowl. Serve with toothpicks or on plates. Will serve 15 to 20 people.

Louise Henshaw's
Hot Asparagus Triangles
They taste like little souffles

1 loaf thinly-sliced white or
   wheat bread
1 (10-ounce) can asparagus,
   drained
1 (8-ounce) package cream
   cheese, softened
2 hard boiled eggs, sieved

Juice of 1 lemon
Seasoning salt to taste
3–4 tablespoons butter,
   softened
1/3–1/2 cup Parmesan cheese,
   grated

Trim crust from day-old bread. Gently mash asparagus a little and cut into large pieces. Mix remainder of ingredients and stir the asparagus into the mixture, just until well mixed (the asparagus should be chunky, not smooth).

Butter one side of each slice of bread. Spread asparagus mixture between two slices buttered bread. Butter outside of sandwiches and sprinkle with Parmesan cheese. Cut into triangles. Place on a greased baking sheet. Bake in a preheated 400° oven until they are brown. Turn once to be sure other side is brown.

Triangles may be frozen before adding cheese and butter on top. Thaw before baking. Makes approximately 20 triangles.

Emily's Toasted Pecans
Give as gifts

4 cups pecan halves
1/4 pound, unsalted butter,
   sliced in small pieces

1 teaspoon salt
1/8 teaspoon black pepper

Preheat oven to 350°. Line cookie sheet with foil. Spread pecans on foil in a single layer. Scatter butter, salt and pepper over pecans. Bake 15 minutes. Stir pecans and taste to see if you need more salt. Cook 5 more minutes. Check again; taste, stir and cook 5 more minutes. Pecans should take a total of approximately 25 minutes to roast. Serve 35–40 people.

 Strawberry Flower: Make cuts lengthwise from tip almost to stem in a large berry. Spread petals. Place a smaller whole berry, tip up, in the center.

Almond Cheesecake

Glorious flavor, creamy and rich

40 vanilla wafers
¾ cup slivered almonds, toasted
1⅓ cups sugar plus 1 table-spoon, divided
⅓ cup butter, melted
3 (8-ounce) packages cream cheese, softened
4 large eggs
⅓ cup heavy cream
¼ cup plus 1 tablespoon amaretto liqueur, divided

2 teaspoons vanilla extract, divided
2 (8-ounce) cartons sour cream
⅓ cup sliced almonds, toasted
1 cup fresh strawberries, sliced
2 Kiwi fruit, sliced
1 recipe Oatmeal Crisps (page 33)

Combine vanilla wafers, slivered almonds and ⅓ cup sugar in food processor. Pulse until crushed. Add butter and blend. Press mixture into bottom and 1¾ inches up the sides of a lightly greased springform pan.

Combine cream cheese and 1 cup sugar. Beat until light and fluffy. Add eggs, one at a time, beating well after each addition. Add cream, ¼ cup amaretto and 1 teaspoon vanilla. Beat well. Pour into crust. Bake in a preheated 350° oven for 30 minutes. Reduce heat to 225° and bake 1 hour. Cool in pan on rack for 5 minutes.

Combine 1 teaspoon vanilla, sour cream, 1 tablespoon sugar and 1 tablespoon amaretto. Spread evenly over warm cake. Return to oven and bake 5 minutes.

Cool in pan on rack 30 minutes. Gently run a knife around edge of pan. Let cool completely in pan on rack. Cover and chill 8 hours.

Remove sides of pan and garnish with a ring of sliced almonds and a nosegay of Kiwi fruit and strawberries. Serve with Oatmeal Crisp Cookies (omit the cinnamon). Guests spread cheesecake and fruit on the cookie.

MORNING PARTIES WITH HEART AND SOUL

Take a Shoppers' Break with Us
Come for Brunch to Meet
Our Weekend Guests
It's Cold Outside! Come for Soup!

People are usually hungrier at a morning party than in late afternoon. If the event is scheduled for around 11 a.m., chances are strong that the hors d'oeuvres will serve as lunch for many guests. Keep this in mind when planning the menu, and include a variety of offerings. If the party is for ladies only, make it elegant by garnishing trays with fresh flowers or herbs. This is the time for a beautiful presentation such as the Vegetable Tree with Hummus.

Since the new trend is to serve less alcohol, especially in the daytime, soup makes a wonderful choice for a beverage. If the soup is cold, a glass pitcher is a more practical serving piece than a punch bowl. A soup tureen is the ideal choice for a hot soup. Guests can easily help themselves, eliminating the necessity of having someone to serve. A morning party is a heartwarming time to entertain. Energy levels are high and people are in the mood for a good time.

Take a Shoppers' Break with Us

Marion's White Christmas Soup
Poinsettia Beverage
Deviled Ham Spirals
Sandy's Spinach Dip
Charlotte Charles' Lump Crabmeat Dip
Parsley and Chive Egg Salad
Vegetable Tree with Hummus
Peppermint Meringues
Peanut Clusters

Marion's White Christmas Soup

Garnish with chopped red and green peppers

1 medium onion, chopped
¼ cup butter or margarine
5 pounds russet potatoes,
  peeled and cubed
8 cups chicken broth
1 teaspoon ground cumin
¼–½ cup coarsely chopped
  pickled jalapenos and
  juice

Pinch of baking soda to
  prevent curdling
4 cups evaporated milk
Salt and pepper to taste
Garnish: sour cream and
  chopped red and green
  peppers

In a large stock pot, sauté onion in butter or margarine until just tender. Add potatoes, chicken broth, and cumin. Cover and cook until potatoes are tender, about 20–30 minutes. When done, add jalapenos, soda, and evaporated milk. Coarsely mash potatoes with potato masher.

Stir well and taste for salt and pepper. Simmer for 15 minutes, stirring frequently. Garnish with a dollop of sour cream and chopped red and green peppers. Serves 16–18.

Poinsettia Beverage

A cup of cheer to toast the holidays

3 cups lemon-lime soft
  drink, chilled
3 cups cranberry juice
  cocktail, chilled

½ cup orange liqueur (or 2
  teaspoons orange extract)
1 teaspoon almond extract

In a 2-quart pitcher, stir together all ingredients. Pour into crystal goblets. To garnish, drop a few fresh cranberries into each goblet. Makes 8 (6-ounce) servings.

Deviled Ham Spirals

Serve these bite-sized treats on toothpicks

1 (6-ounce) package sliced
  smoked ham
¼ cup unsalted butter,
  softened
1 tablespoon honey
¼ teaspoon ground cloves

2 tablespoons coarse-grain
  mustard
3 tablespoons mayonnaise
3 tablespoons onion, finely
  chopped
Flour tortillas

Process ham in a food processor until finely chopped. Add butter, honey, cloves, mustard and mayonnaise and blend until smooth. Spoon mixture into a bowl. Stir in the onion. Spread on flour tortillas, roll up and slice into pinwheels. Serve on toothpicks. Makes approximately 40–50.

Sandy's Spinach Dip

Tastes even better the next day

1 package frozen chopped
  spinach
1 can artichoke hearts,
  drained
1 cup Parmesan cheese

1 cup Monterey Jack cheese,
  grated
1 cup mayonnaise
Red pepper flakes to taste

Cook frozen spinach and drain. Combine with remaining ingredients. Bake at 375° for 30 minutes.

Charlotte Charles' Lump Crabmeat Dip

Elegant, delicious specialty from a legendary caterer

1 stick butter
1 cup flour
1 bunch green onions, including tops, chopped
3 cups half and half cream or evaporated milk
½ teaspoon salt
½ teaspoon lemon pepper
¼ teaspoon dried basil
2 teaspoons Worcestershire sauce

¼ teaspoon cayenne pepper or ⅛ teaspoon Tabasco sauce
1 (4-ounce) can pimientos, chopped
1 large can mushrooms or ½ pound fresh mushrooms, sliced
2 pounds fresh or canned lump crabmeat
½ cup sherry

Melt butter, gradually add flour, and stir until smooth. Sauté onions until transparent. Add cream or evaporated milk and cook, stirring constantly, until thickened. Stir in seasonings, pimientos, and mushrooms. Fold in crabmeat. Add sherry. Serves 70.

Parsley and Chive Egg Salad

From Chef Stephanie Palumbos at the Hill House Restaurant in Terry.

8 hard boiled eggs
½ bunch chives cut into small rings
½ bunch Italian parsley cut into thin strips

1 cup mayonnaise
1 tablespoon Dijon mustard
Salt and pepper to taste
1 loaf thin sliced white bread

Chop eggs by hand into small chunks. Mix all ingredients together and season with salt and pepper to taste. Make sandwiches; trim crusts; cut into triangles. Makes 22.

Vegetable Tree with Hummus

A festive holiday presentation

10-inch styrofoam cone
Florist picks
A variety of lettuces, broccoli florets, cherry tomatoes

Dippers: asparagus spears, cauliflower, carrots, broccoli

Cover the cone with lettuces. Secure with florist picks. Decorate with broccoli florets and cherry tomatoes like a Christmas tree. Place on a tray surrounded by vegetable dippers. Serve with Hummus.

Hummus

A Middle Eastern dip with a nutty flavor

**1 (16-ounce) can chick-peas
or garbanzo beans,
drained**
3 cloves garlic, minced

⅓ cup tahini paste
¼ cup lemon juice
⅛ teaspoon salt
Cayenne

Drain the chick-peas, saving liquid. Purée the chick-peas in a food processor. Add the garlic, tahini and lemon juice, processing until creamy. If needed, thin with a small amount of reserved liquid. Season with salt. Pour into a dish and dust lightly with cayenne. May be served with vegetables or pita chips.

Peppermint Meringues

Chips of peppermint candy give them a holiday look

**4 egg whites (room tempera-
ture)**
½ teaspoon cream of tartar
¼ teaspoon salt

1 cup sugar, sifted
**1 teaspoon peppermint
extract**
Peppermint candy sticks

Preheat oven to 225°. Beat egg whites, cream of tartar and salt on low speed until foamy. Increase speed on mixer to medium and beat until soft peaks form. Turn to high speed and add sugar, one tablespoon at a time. Continue beating until stiff, but not dry. Add peppermint extract. Cover 2 cookie sheets with foil.

Drop mixture by teaspoon onto foil. Bake 1 hour, turn off oven and leave meringues inside at least 4 hours or overnight. When cool, crush peppermint sticks by placing them in a plastic bag and hitting them with a hammer. Sprinkle candy bits over meringues. Makes 55–60.

Peanut Clusters

Make extras for gifts

1 pound almond bark
12 ounces chocolate chips
**2 (1-ounce) bars bittersweet
chocolate**

**2 (16-ounce) jars dry roasted
whole salted peanuts**

Melt first three ingredients in a Crock Pot or double boiler. When melted, stir in two jars peanuts. Drop onto waxed paper with a teaspoon.

Come for Brunch to Meet Our Weekend Guests

Welsh Rabbit with Condiments
Sausage Balls with Jezebel Sauce
Aunt Katie's Egg Mousse
Creole Cream Cheese with Fruit
Emily Davis' Orange Blueberry Bread
with Honey-Orange Butter
Spice Cake Squares
Oatmeal Shortbread Tartlets with
Lemon Curd and Kiwi

Welsh Rabbit with Condiments

Guests fill toast cups with delicacies and Welsh Rabbit

**¾ cup stale beer, room
temperature
1 tablespoon butter
1 pound sharp Cheddar
cheese, grated
1 teaspoon dry mustard
½ teaspoon Worcestershire
sauce
⅛ teaspoon cayenne pepper**

**½ teaspoon salt
1 egg, slightly beaten
Condiments: Lump crabmeat
slivers of country ham
asparagus tips
chopped hard boiled eggs
green onions
black olives
tomatoes**

Have all ingredients at room temperature. Open beer 8 hours in advance. In the top of a double boiler, melt butter over hot, not boiling water. It is important that rabbit never boils. Keep the water only hot enough to melt the ingredients. Add cheese and all but 1 tablespoon beer. Cook stirring constantly until cheese melts.

Combine seasonings with the tablespoon of beer and stir into the cheese. Stir in slightly beaten egg. Keep warm over hot water in the bottom pan of the chafing dish. Do not use the flame. It is better to reheat than to risk boiling and the cheese separating. Make in batches if you need more. If your ingredients are ready, it will not take long.

Serve with Toast Cups on page 20 and place separate bowls of crabmeat, ham, asparagus tips, chopped hard boiled eggs, green onions, black olives and chopped fresh tomatoes around the chafing dish. Guests fill the toast cups with Welsh Rabbit and Condiments of their choice.

Sausage Balls with Jezebel Sauce

A favorite that is exceptionally easy

1 pound hot bulk sausage
1 (8-ounce) package extra
  sharp cheddar cheese,
  shredded

2 cups biscuit mix

Mix sausage and cheese together. Thoroughly knead biscuit mix into sausage and cheese. Shape into small balls the size of a marble. Bake in preheated 350° oven for 20 minutes. Serve with or without Jezebel sauce. Makes 80–90 balls.

Jezebel Sauce

Delicious with pork, beef or chicken

1 (12-ounce) jar pineapple
  preserves
1 (12-ounce) jar apple jelly
1 (5-ounce) jar prepared
  horseradish

3 tablespoons dry mustard
1 teaspoon black pepper

Mix all ingredients. Store in refrigerator. Will keep indefinitely.

Aunt Katie's Egg Mousse

Serve it Savannah style with caviar

**1 tablespoons unflavored
    gelatin**
2 cups chicken broth
**6 eggs, hard boiled and
    quartered**

½–1 teaspoon curry powder
⅛ teaspoon white pepper
**2 (2-ounce) jars caviar,
    chilled**

Soak gelatin in ½ cup chicken broth for 5 minutes. In the top of a double boiler, bring it to a boil and simmer, stirring until gelatin is completely dissolved. Cool slightly.

Place gelatin, the remainder of the chicken broth, egg quarters, curry power and white pepper in a blender or food processor. Blend and cool. Pour into a buttered or oiled mold. Cover and refrigerate for 4 hours or overnight. May be made 2 days in advance.

When ready to serve, embellish the mousse that has been placed on a serving plate with chilled caviar. Will serve 6–8 people.

Creole Cream Cheese with Fruit

Delicately flavored—perfect with fruit and bread

**1 (16-ounce) carton large
    curd cottage cheese**
**1 cup whipping cream,
    whipped**
**¼ cup confectioners' sugar,
    or to taste**

**2 tablespoons orange peel,
    shredded**
Fresh seasonal fruit
**French bread, sliced and
    toasted**

Purée cottage cheese in blender or processor, using on and off turns until smooth yet retains some texture.

Whip cream. Add sugar and peel. Gently fold into cottage cheese. Pack into bowl or crock. Refrigerate overnight. To serve, set crock on platter and surround with fruit and toast.

 Melons are ripe when they feel heavy in hand and the flesh around the stem gives slightly when pressed.

Emily Davis' Orange Blueberry Bread
Serve with Honey-Orange Butter

2 tablespoons butter (no substitutions)	**1 egg**
¼ cup boiling water	**1 cup sugar**
½ cup fresh orange juice (approximately 1½–2 oranges)	**2 cups flour**
	1 teaspoon baking powder
	¼ teaspoon baking soda
4 teaspoons orange rind, grated	**½ teaspoon salt**
	1 cup fresh blueberries

TOPPING:

2 tablespoons fresh lemon juice (1 lemon)	**2 tablespoons honey**
	1 teaspoon grated lemon rind

Place butter in a small bowl. Pour in boiling water and stir until melted. Add orange juice and rind. In another bowl beat egg with sugar until light.

Into a large bowl sift the dry ingredients. Alternately add orange mixture and egg mixture to dry ingredients, beating until smooth. Carefully fold in berries. Pour into a greased loaf pan. Bake in a preheated 325° oven 1 hour and 10 minutes. Test for doneness with a toothpick. Turn onto a wire rack.

Mix together lemon juice, honey, and lemon rind. Spoon over hot loaf. Will freeze. Makes 1 loaf.

Orange Honey Butter
Wonderful with Bueberry Orange Bread

1 cup butter, softened	**2½ teaspoons grated orange zest**
½ cup honey	
6 tablespoons orange juice	

Beat butter until fluffy. Slowly add orange juice and zest, mixing well. Press into a decorative butter mold such as a heart shape mold or into a pretty ramekin. Serve with the Blueberry Orange Bread.

Spice Cake Squares with Baked-on-Icing

Modern convenience, old-fashioned taste

1 cup shortening	**1 teaspoon cloves, ground**
2 cups light brown sugar	**1 teaspoon cinnamon**
2 whole eggs	**1 cup buttermilk**
2 egg yolks	**4 egg whites, stiffly beaten**
2²/₃ cups all-purpose flour	**2 cups brown sugar**
1 teaspoon soda	**½ cup pecans or walnuts,**
1 teaspoon baking powder	**chopped**

Cream shortening. Add sugar and eggs. Sift dry ingredients together and add alternately to the batter with the buttermilk, beginning with dry ingredients. Beat 2 minutes. Place in an oblong cake pan.

Beat egg whites until stiff. With the mixer, slowly add the brown sugar. Spread over the dough in the cake pan. Sprinkle chopped nuts over the top and bake at 300° about 1 hour and 15 minutes. Test for doneness. Cuts into 36 small squares.

Oatmeal Shortbread Tartlets with Lemon Curd and Kiwi

Combines old favorites into a few luscious bites

SHORTBREAD SHELLS:

½ cup unsalted butter, softened	**¼ teaspoon salt**
	Lemon Curd (page 74)
¹/₃ cup sugar	**2 kiwi fruit**
¼ cup all-purpose flour	
½ cup old-fashioned rolled oats	

Cream butter and sugar until light and fluffy. Mix flour, oats, and salt. Blend with butter mixture until just combined. Press rounded teaspoons of dough into the bottom and up the sides of buttered gem pans or mini muffin tins. Chill 15 minutes.

Bake in the middle of a 350° preheated oven 10–12 minutes or until they are golden brown around the edge. Cool 5 minutes and loosen with the tip of a sharp knife. Cool on wire racks. May be placed in an airtight container for 2 days.

Peel kiwi. Slice them ⅛-inch thick. Quarter each slice. Fill shortbread shells with a rounded teaspoon of curd and top with a piece of kiwi. Makes 35 tartlets.

It's Cold Outside— Come for Soup!

Pea and Ham Soup
Shrimp Bisque
Bloody Mary Gazpacho
Sweet Potato Biscuits
Mr. Louis' Banana-Nut Muffins
Tessie's Five O'Clock Tea Muffins
Angela Lang's Cheese Torte
Spinach Artichoke Squares
Outback Biscuits

Pea and Ham Soup
May be served hot or cold

2 cans pea soup
2 cups milk
1 (4-ounce) can deviled ham
1 teaspoon dried basil
1 teaspoon dried dill
1 tablespoon grated lemon rind
Salt and pepper to taste

Combine first 5 ingredients in blender for 1 minute. Add lemon rind, salt and pepper and blend 8 seconds. Makes 4 servings.

Shrimp Bisque
Smooth and flavorful, ideal comfort food

2 cans tiny shrimp with juice
3 tablespoons butter
3 tablespoons flour
1 quart milk
1 teaspoon salt
3 tablespoons dry sherry
¼ teaspoon paprika
¼ teaspoon white pepper
¼ teaspoon nutmeg
1 teaspoon Worcestershire sauce
¼–½ teaspoon Cajun seasoning
1 tablespoon parsley flakes

Process shrimp and juice in food processor for a few seconds. Make a smooth cream sauce with butter, flour, milk and salt. Add spices and seasonings and bring to a boil slowly, stirring constantly. Lower heat and cook 2 minutes, stirring constantly. Add parsley flakes, processed shrimp with juice and sherry. Makes 6 servings.

Bloody Mary Gazpacho

Serve in a tall glass pitcher

7 medium tomatoes
3 slices bread
1 garlic clove
3 tablespoons white wine vinegar
⅓ cup olive oil
4 cups tomato juice
2 cups canned beef broth
2 teaspoons dried basil
1 teaspoon celery seed

1 medium bell pepper
1 medium purple onion
1 small cucumber
3 tablespoons lime juice
2 teaspoons Worcestershire sauce
¼ cup vodka (or to taste)
1 teaspoon salt
½ teaspoon pepper

Peel and fourth the tomatoes. Tear bread into small chunks. Process tomatoes, bread and garlic until blended. With the motor running, pour vinegar and oil through feed tube and process until puréed. Pour into a large bowl. Add tomato juice, broth, basil and celery seed.

Quarter and seed the bell pepper. Quarter and peel the onion. Peel and cut cucumber into chunks, removing seeds with a spoon. Process vegetables until coarsely chopped, and add to tomato mixture. Stir in lime juice, Worcestershire sauce, vodka, salt and pepper. Chill until serving time.

Sweet Potato Biscuits

So flavorful you don't need to butter them

1 egg, slightly beaten
1 cup cooked, mashed sweet potatoes
¼–½ cup sugar
2 tablespoons butter or margarine, softened

3 tablespoons shortening
2 cups self-rising flour, approximately

Combine egg, sweet potatoes, sugar, butter and shortening in a mixing bowl; mix well. Stir in enough flour to make a soft dough. (Dough will be softer than regular biscuit dough.) Turn out on floured surface; knead lightly a few times. Roll to ¼-inch thickness. Cut with a 2-inch biscuit cutter. Place on ungreased baking sheet and bake at 350° about 15 minutes. Yield: about 16 (2-inch) biscuits.

Mr. Louis' Banana-Nut Muffins

From the pastry chef at Emeril's in New Orleans

2 cups all-purpose flour
1 tablespoon baking powder
2 eggs
¾ cup sugar
¼ cup oil
¾ cup light cream
1 tablespoon orange zest
1 banana, finely chopped
1 cup toasted walnuts, chopped

Sift dry ingredients together. Combine eggs, sugar, oil, cream and orange zest. Mix banana and nuts in a separate bowl with 2 tablespoons of dry ingredients. Add wet ingredients to dry ingredients and fold in nuts and bananas. Grease muffin tins and pour in batter. Bake in preheated 400° oven for 10 minutes. Makes 1½ dozen.

Angela Lang's Cheese Torte

Decorate with basil leaves and red pepper strips

24 ounces cream cheese
1 cup grated Parmesan cheese
2½ teaspoons minced garlic
2½ teaspoons dried basil (or 5 teaspoons fresh)
½ teaspoon pepper
2 roasted red peppers
½ cup pinenuts (may substitute pecans or almonds), toasted
1 teaspoon oil

Cream together cream cheese, Parmesan cheese and seasonings. Bake red peppers at 500° until black, then place in plastic bag. Seal 15 minutes. Remove peppers, peel, seed and chop.

Line a 6-inch salad mold with plastic wrap, add 1 teaspoon oil and grease well. Place a layer of cream cheese, nuts, cream cheese, roasted red peppers, cream cheese. Refrigerate for several hours. Serve with crackers.

Tessie's Five O'Clock Tea Muffins

A very old recipe from Mrs. C. R. Day of Vicksburg

4 eggs, slightly beaten
2 cups dark brown sugar
2 cups flour, sifted twice
½ teaspoon salt
1 teaspoon baking powder
1 cup pecans, chopped
Confectioners' sugar

Mix all ingredients together except confectioners' sugar until dry ingredients are well moistened. Scoop batter into lined mini-muffin tins. Bake at 325° for 15 minutes. Cool. Sift confectioners' sugar over muffins. Makes 45–48.

Spinach Artichoke Squares

Cook ahead and freeze

CRUST:

4 cups sharp cheddar
  cheese, grated
1½ cups flour

1 teaspoon salt
½ teaspoon dry mustard
1 cup butter, melted

Combine dry ingredients. Stir in butter and mix well. Spray 9x12-inch glass baking dish with cooking spray. Press cheese mixture into dish.

FILLING:

2 (10-ounce) packages
  frozen chopped spinach,
  thawed, drained and
  squeezed
¼ cup lemon juice
1 cup light cream
1 medium onion, chopped
½ cup canned sliced mush-
  rooms

½ teaspoon salt
¼ teaspoon basil
¼ teaspoon oregano
½ teaspoon pepper
2 eggs, beaten, slightly
1 (14-ounce) can artichoke
  hearts, drained and sliced
Grated Parmesan cheese

Preheat oven to 400°. Mix together everything except Parmesan cheese. Pour into crust. Sprinkle with Parmesan. Bake at 400° for 15 minutes. Reduce heat to 350° and bake approximately 30 minute until brown. Cool thoroughly and refrigerate for at least 2 hours before cutting into squares. Warm before serving. Make approximately 30 squares.

Outback Biscuits

Popular snack in Australia and New Zealand

1 teaspoon baking soda
2 tablespoons boiling water
1 cup butter, melted
1 tablespoon cane syrup

1½ cups of old-fashioned
  oats
1½ cups brown sugar
1½ cups flour
1½ cups coconut

Dissolve soda in boiling water. Stir in melted butter and syrup. Add dry ingredients and stir well. Roll into ¾-inch balls and place on greased baking sheets. Flatten balls with your hand. Bake in 350° pre-heated oven for 8–10 minutes until brown. Cool well before storing. Makes 5 dozen.

TEATIME—THE LOVELIEST TIME OF DAY

"Sip Tea 'N' See" Our New Baby

We Request the Pleasure of Your Company for High Tea

Join in the Fun at Our Membership Tea

Let's Take Time To Visit— Join Me for Tea

Late afternoon is not only the most formal time to entertain, but also the most practical. At the hour when your energy sags and you need a pick-up to give you a lift until dinner time, what could be more refreshing than a cup of bracing tea?

Get out your best linens, china and serving pieces for the occasion and grace the house with lovely flowers. Sandwiches, sweets and fruits are the most popular teatime foods, served on trays garnished with flowers. The theme can be anything from a Sip 'N' See Party (to show off a new baby or let friends see your wedding gifts,) to a romantic Valentine's Day Celebration.

Whether you serve tea from a silver service or pour it from a pitcher, your guests will luxuriate in the familiar ritual of one of life's beautiful events.

"Sip 'N' See" Our New Baby

Tressa's Mint Tea for a Crowd
Mushroom Roll-Ups
Parmesan Rounds
Crawfish Mold
Lovett's Inn Cream Scones
Brandied Raisin Mold
with Strawberries
Karen's Coconut Meringues
Mana's Teacakes with Lemon Curd

Tressa's Mint Tea for a Crowd

For a more pronounced lemon taste, add more juice and rind

15½ cups of water, divided
7 tea bags
7 sprigs of mint

Juice of 4 lemons
Rind of 2 lemons
2 cups sugar

Bring 7 cups of water to a boil. Add tea bags, mint, lemon juice, and lemon rind (in large pieces, not grated). Steep for 15 minutes. Mix remaining 8½ cups of water with sugar. Strain tea into sugar water; stirring well. Place in pitcher in the refrigerator. Makes 1 gallon.

Mushroom Roll-ups

Easy to pass, easy to eat

1 family-size loaf white bread
½ pound mushrooms, chopped fine
½ cup butter, melted
3 tablespoons flour

¾ teaspoon salt
¼ teaspoon MSG
1 cup light cream
2 teaspoons chives
1 teaspoon lemon juice

Remove crust from bread, roll flat with rolling pin. Sauté mushrooms in butter. Blend in flour, salt and MSG. Gradually stir in cream and cook until thick. Add chives and lemon juice. Spread mixture over bread slices and roll up. Cut in half and toast in 400° oven until brown. Makes 40.

Parmesan Rounds

These tasty pick-ups disappear fast

1 cup Parmesan cheese, grated
1 cup flour, sifted
7 tablespoons sour cream
¼ cup butter
½ teaspoon salt
Paprika

Mix together all ingredients except paprika. Chill for 30 minutes. Roll out dough about ¼-inch thick on a lightly floured board. Cut into rounds with a small biscuit cutter (or the lip of a narrow glass). Place on ungreased baking sheet and bake in a 350° oven for 15 minutes or until done. Sprinkle with paprika. Warm slightly in oven before serving. Makes 2½ dozen.

Crawfish Mold

Shrimp are equally good in this delicious mold

1 pound crawfish tails, cooked
½ cup water
1 envelope unflavored gelatin
1 (8-ounce) package cream cheese
1 cup heavy cream
⅓ cup mayonnaise
1 tablespoon parsley
1 bunch green onion tops, chopped
¼ cup capers
½ cup green olives, sliced
1 teaspoon Worcestershire sauce
½ teaspoon salt
½ teaspoon pepper

Dice crawfish into thirds and set aside. Heat water and stir in gelatin until dissolved. Blend cream cheese in mixer with cream. Add gelatin mixture, mayonnaise, parsley, onion tops, capers, olives and seasonings. Beat until well combined. Pour into a 5 or 6-cup mold that has been greased with no stick cooking spray. Serve with crackers.

Lovett's Inn Cream Scones

From a country inn in Franconia, New Hampshire

2 cups flour
1 tablespoon baking powder
½ teaspoon salt
¼ cup sugar
¼ cup dried cranberries
¼ cup dried pears, chopped

¼ cup dried apricots,
  chopped
1¼ cups heavy cream
Glaze:
  3 tablespoons butter,
  melted
  2 tablespoons sugar

Combine dry ingredients in a bowl with sugar, mixing well. Add dried fruit. With a fork, stir in cream until dough holds together.

Knead dough on a lightly floured board for a short time. Pat into a 10-inch circle. Spread melted butter on top and sides and sprinkle with sugar. Cut into 12 wedges and place on a greased baking sheet about 1 inch apart. (May cut dough into rounds with a biscuit cutter. Makes 2½ dozen rounds). Bake in a 425° oven for approximately 15 minutes.

Serve with Mock Clotted Cream (page 79) and raspberry preserves.

Brandied Raisin Mold with Strawberries

Looks pretty in ring mold filled with berries

2 packages unflavored
  gelatin
½ cup cold water
24 ounces cream cheese,
  softened
2 sticks butter, very soft
1 cup sour cream
1 cup sugar
2 cups white raisins

Enough brandy to cover
  raisins (soak overnight or
  up to 2 years)
2 cups slivered almonds
Grated rind of 4 lemons
Strawberries

Dissolve gelatin in ½ cup water in double boiler. Combine next 4 ingredients in large bowl. When gelatin is dissolved, combine with cream cheese mixture. Drain raisins. Add raisins, almonds, and lemon rind; mix well by hand. Put in greased 2-quart mold. Chill at least overnight or longer. You can use three packages of gelatin to insure stiffness. Serve with strawberries.

Karen's Coconut Meringues
Light and airy, with a hint of chocolate

4 egg whites
¼ teaspoon cream of tartar
1 cup sugar
1 cup pecans, chopped

½ cup coconut
1-ounce square semisweet
chocolate, finely chopped
½ teaspoon almond extract

Beat egg whites and cream of tartar at high speed until soft peaks form. Add sugar gradually beating well after addition until whites are firm and glossy. Turn mixer to low, and fold in last four ingredients. Drop by teaspoons onto foil-lined cookie sheets. Bake 40 minutes at 250°. Cool. Store in airtight containers. Makes 6 dozen.

Mana's Teacakes
Freeze in rolls; bake when needed

2 sticks butter or margarine,
softened
1 cup sugar
2 teaspoons lemon rind (or
more, to taste)

1 egg
3 cups flour

Cream margarine, sugar and lemon rind until smooth. Add egg and mix well. Add flour gradually. Roll into three logs, wrap in waxed paper, then in foil. Freeze. Take out of freezer when you want fresh-baked cookies. Thaw slightly, slice and bake at 350° for approximately 10 minutes. Makes 8 dozen small cookies. Serve with lemon curd.

Lemon Curd
Keeps one month in refrigerator

4 lemons, juice and grated
rind
1 cup sugar

½ cup butter
6 egg yolks
2 whole eggs

Combine lemon juice, rind, sugar and butter in a saucepan. Place over low heat until mixture is boiling and sugar is dissolved. Beat yolks and eggs until combined. While continuing to beat, add a thin stream of the hot liquid. Cook mixture over low heat, stirring constantly until thick. Remove from heat and stir for 4 minutes longer. Cool, cover and refrigerate. Serve in a dish with cookies around it. Place cheese knife on dish for serving.

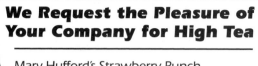

We Request the Pleasure of Your Company for High Tea

Mary Hufford's Strawberry Punch
Hot Tea
Creamed Chipped Beef with Toast Cups
Rolled Watercress Sandwiches
Saga Blue Walnut Spirals
Bacon, Lettuce and Love Apple Rounds
My Cousin's Lemon Scones
Chocolate Dipped Candied Citrus Peels
Apricots with Mascarpone
Chocolate Covered Cherry Bon Bons
Pruitt's Almond Bon Bons
Orange Liqueur Cake

Mary Hufford's Strawberry Punch

The perfect punch to serve at a large tea

4 (12-ounce) packages sliced strawberries
1 cup sugar
4 bottles Rosé wine
4 (6-ounce) cans frozen lemonade, undiluted

2 large bottles club soda
Strawberries for garnish, or a strawberry and mint ice ring

Thaw berries and mix in sugar. Pour one bottle Rosé wine over mixture and let it stand, covered, for one hour. Strain into a bowl. Discard berries or use over ice cream or pound cake.

Add lemonade. Stir until dissolved. Add wine and soda before serving. Makes 33 cups of punch or ½ gallon.

To make ice ring: Arrange whole strawberries and mint leaves in a 6-cup ring mold. Pour a thin layer of water over fruit and leaves, being careful not to disturb them. Freeze until firm, about 2 hours. Add very cold water one or two times, freezing after each addition.

Hot Tea

Both hot tea and punch are served at formal teas

Darjeeling tea or tea of your choice
Bottled water
Sugar cubes

Lemon, thinly sliced and cut in half
Light cream or milk

Essential ingredients for good tea are: good leaves, fresh water and timing.

Place 1 teaspoon of tea for each cup plus 1 for the pot into a wire mesh infuser or tea ball. It is better to have tea too strong than too weak. If too strong, just add hot water. If too weak, throw it out and start over. Warm the pot with a rinsing of hot water just before pouring the fresh water for tea.

Fill kettle with fresh bottled water. If you are using water from the tap, let it flow a few minutes. Do not use tap water if there are too many chemicals or minerals, such as iron. Bring the water to a boil over a medium flame. Just as the water reaches a full rolling boil, remove from the flame.

Pour the water onto the leaves. Cover and let it stand for 5 minutes. Do not leave the leaves in longer than 6 minutes.

At a formal tea, it is considered an honor for a guest to be asked to serve. First the server will ask each guest if they would like sugar, one lump or two? If yes, she will place it in the empty cup with small sugar tongs. Then she will ask if they would like lemon or cream. The cream or milk is poured before the tea. If they prefer lemon, offer a small plate with thinly sliced lemon and a small fork. After handing the cup to the guest, offer hot water for those who like a weaker tea.

Creamed Chipped Beef

Serve from a chafing dish with toast cups

2 ribs celery, minced
1 onion, minced
¼ cup butter
3 tablespoons flour
2 cups light cream
5 ounces dried chipped beef, shredded

½ cup fresh or frozen green peas
White pepper
Toast Cups (page 20)

Sauté celery and onions in butter for 3 minutes. Add flour and stir for 3 minutes. Remove pan from heat and whisk in the cream. Return to heat and cook over medium low heat for 2 minutes. Add beef and peas, cook another 3 minutes. Add salt and pepper to taste.

Creamed chipped beef is also served with scrambled eggs for an elegant brunch.

Rolled Watercress Sandwiches

The best of the dainty tea sandwiches

1 loaf thinly sliced white bread, fresh as possible
6 tablespoons butter, softened
⅓ cup watercress sprigs, finely chopped
1 teaspoon green onion, finely chopped

½ teaspoon Worcestershire sauce
¼ teaspoon salt
Black pepper, ground
Watercress sprigs, about 64 leaves

Buy the freshest bread possible. Trim away crust and roll with a rolling pin.

Combine all ingredients except whole watercress sprigs. Spread on bread slices and roll. Place seam side down in container. Refrigerate up to 24 hours by covering with waxed paper, then a damp towel, then plastic wrap. Bring to room temperature to serve. Cut each roll in half and tuck a watercress spring in each end. Makes 32.

 Emergency breadsticks: Slice hamburger buns lengthwise into desired size (bottoms in half- tops in thirds). Dip in melted butter. Sprinkle with sesame or poppy seeds. Bake 10 to 12 minutes in a 350° oven.

Saga Blue Walnut Spirals
Decorate with pansies or other fresh flowers

1 cup (about ²/₃ pound) Saga
  blue cheese, softened
½ cup walnuts, chopped
¼ cup parsley leaves,
  minced

1½ teaspoons fresh lemon
  juice
¼ teaspoon ground white
  pepper
8 large flour tortillas

Combine the ingredients and blend with a fork until they are of spreading consistency. Spread mixture on each of the tortillas and roll them jelly-roll fashion. Secure by wrapping them tightly in plastic wrap. Chill at least two hours or up to 2 days.

To serve, cut the tortillas into ¼-inch thick slices with a serrated knife. Arrange on a plate and garnish with pansies or other flowers and parsley or watercress. Makes 1½ cups filling or approximately 60 spirals.

Bacon, Lettuce and Love Apple Rounds
Cherry tomatoes add color to these little sandwiches

20 slices thin white sandwich bread
Mayonnaise
10 slices bacon, cooked crisp

3 or 4 large lettuce leaves
10 cherry tomatoes, halved,
  seeded and drained
Salt and pepper to taste

Use a 2½-inch doughnut cutter with a removable center hole cutter. Cut 10 bread rounds with a hole in the center. Remove the center of the cutter and cut 10 bread rounds without the hole. Toast lightly.

Spread all 20 rounds with mayonnaise. Cut lettuce leaves in 2½-inch rounds and place one leaf on each of the 10 whole bread rounds. Break bacon into large pieces and place one slice on each piece of lettuce. Next place the bread round with the hole in the center on top of the bacon. Place a cherry tomato half, cut side down, in the hole.

To serve, have ingredients assembled and put together not more than 15 minutes in advance of serving. Makes 10 sandwiches.

My Cousin's Lemon Scones
As wonderful as they sound

2½ cups all-purpose flour
1 tablespoon lemon peel,
  freshly grated
1 tablespoon baking powder
½ teaspoon salt
8 tablespoons cold unsalted
  butter, cut into pieces

⅓ cup granulated sugar
⅔ cup milk
2 teaspoons fresh lemon
  juice
2 tablespoons sugar
Raspberry Butter
Mock Clotted Cream

Preheat oven to 425°. Mix well the flour, grated lemon peel, baking powder and salt. Cut in butter with a pastry blender until it looks like fine granules. Add sugar and mix. Slowly add milk and stir until a soft dough forms. Roll dough into a ball and place on a lightly floured board. Knead 10–12 times.

Mix lemon juice and 2 tablespoons sugar. Before baking, top each scone with ¼ teaspoon.

To make triangular scones cut dough in half. Knead each half into a ball. Turn smooth side up. Pat or roll into a 6-inch circle. Cut each circle into 6 to 8 wedges. Place on an ungreased cookie sheet slightly apart for crisp sides.

Top with lemon juice and sugar. Bake 12 minutes or until medium brown on top. Cool in wire rack covered loosely with a cloth. Serve with Raspberry Butter and Mock Clotted Cream. Makes 12–16 triangles or 18 (2-inch) rounds.

Raspberry Butter

1 pound butter, softened
½ pint fresh raspberries,
  washed, room temperature

1 teaspoon lemon zest

Have all ingredients at room temperature. Whip butter with a mixer until soft. Whip in lemon zest. Slowly and gently add raspberries.

Mock Clotted Cream
Serve with fruit as well as with scones

1 cup heavy cream, whipped
                             ¼ cup sour cream

Beat cream and sour cream together until soft peaks form. Serve in a white bowl or individually, in oversized egg cups or on the plate with a scone.

Clotted cream is a dense, rich cream found only in some regions of England. An English tradition with scones at tea, it is served extensively in England with fruit, as well as scones. Our recipe makes a good substitute for the popular thick cream.

Chocolate Dipped Candied Citrus Peels

Leaving the white pith on makes it easier and tastier

1 pink grapefruit
3 large oranges with thick shiny skin
2 large lemons
2 large limes
1 ½ cups sugar, plus extra sugar to roll the peels in

8 ounces semisweet chocolate
4 ounce unsweetened chocolate
2 teaspoons vegetable oil
48 pieces candied fruit peel

Keep a plastic bag in your freezer to store fruit peels in as you use the fruit.

Make incisions through the skin of each piece of fruit to separate it into 6 sections. Separate the skin from the fruit.

Place the peels in a pot and cover with cold water. Bring to a strong boil and boil for 30 seconds. Pour into a colander, rinse fruit and pot under cold water. Repeat procedure one more time.

Return the peels to a clean pot for the third time. Add 8 cups water and 1 ½ cups sugar. Boil gently, uncovered, for 1 ½ hours or until the skins are almost transparent and there is just enough thick syrup to coat them.

Cover a cookie sheet with sugar and roll the peels in it until well coated. Let them cool, dry, and harden for several hours or overnight.

Melt semisweet and unsweetened chocolates in the top of a double boiler. Stir in vegetable oil. Do not let chocolate get too hot or it will lose its shininess.

Pour chocolate into a narrow dish or glass. Dip ⅓ of an end of the peel into the chocolate. Lift it and let the excess chocolate drip off.

Place the peel on an oiled tray. Repeat for all the rinds. Let set in the refrigerator for at least 30 minutes. Makes 48.

Apricots with Mascarpone

Beautiful with tea or coffee

4 ounces Mascarpone cheese
¼ cup sour cream
⅛ teaspoon salt

⅛ teaspoon pepper
36 small dried apricot halves
36 cilantro leaves for garnish

Beat cheese, sour cream, salt and pepper until fluffy.

Arrange apricots on serving tray. Place cut side down. Use a pastry bag fitted with a star tip to pipe a rosette of cheese mixture in center of each apricot. Garnish each with a cilantro leaf. Yield 36.

Fruit Caramels

Fruit and nuts combined for a special treat

1 cup figs
1 cup seeded raisins
1 cup dates
1 cup walnuts

1 tablespoon candied orange peel
2 to 4 tablespoons fresh orange juice
Confectioners' sugar

Grind the first five ingredients together in a food processor. Moisten with the orange juice until of good consistency to form into small balls. Roll in confectioners' sugar. Makes about 25 caramels.

Chocolate Covered Cherry Bon Bons

A maraschino cherry is hidden in the cookie

¾ cup confectioners' sugar
½ cup butter or margarine, softened
1 ounce unsweetened chocolate, melted
1 tablespoon vanilla
1½ cups all-purpose flour (do not use self-rising)

⅛ teaspoon salt
24 maraschino cherries, drained and patted dry
Rum (optional)
Chocolate glaze

Heat oven to 350°. Mix sugar, butter, melted chocolate that has been cooled, and vanilla. Work in flour and salt until dough holds together (mix in 1–2 tablespoons milk if dough is dry).

Shape dough around a cherry using a tablespoon. If desired, cherries may be drained and marinated in rum several days before baking cookies. Pat dry before using.

Place cookies 1-inch apart on an ungreased cookie sheet. Bake until set but not brown (12–15 minutes). Cool. Dip top of cookies into glaze. Makes 24 cookies.

CHOCOLATE GLAZE:

1 cup confectioners' sugar
2 tablespoons milk
1 teaspoon vanilla

1 ounce unsweetened chocolate, melted and cooled

Beat together until smooth and of desired consistency. Add more milk, if necessary.

Pruitt's Almond Bon Bons
A very special cookie

¼ pound (1 stick) butter, softened
¼ pound margarine, softened
1½ cups confectioners' sugar
1 egg, beaten
½ teaspoon vanilla extract
½ teaspoon almond extract
2½ cups cake flour
1 teaspoon cream of tartar
1 teaspoon soda
Whole almonds

Thoroughly cream butter, margarine, and confectioners' sugar. Add eggs and extracts. Beat well. Add sifted dry ingredients. Mix well. Chill in refrigerator one hour or longer. Form into small balls. Place on a greased cookie sheet. Flatten slightly and place an almond in the center of each. Bake in a preheated 375° oven 10–12 minutes.

Orange Liqueur Cake
A triumph for tea or coffee

Cake:

1 cup butter
1 cup sugar
3 eggs, separated
1 teaspoon Grand Marnier
2 cups all-purpose flour
1 teaspoon baking powder
1 teaspoon baking soda
1¼ cups sour cream
Grated rind of 1 orange
1 cup walnuts, chopped and toasted

Preheat oven to 350°. Cream butter and sugar until pale and fluffy. Beat in egg yolks, one at a time. Add Grand Marnier. Sift together flour, baking powder, and soda. Add to batter, alternating with sour cream, beginning and ending with dry ingredients. Mix until smooth. Stir in rind and walnuts.

Beat egg whites until stiff. Fold into batter. Pour into a greased tube pan. Bake 50–55 minutes or until cake tests done.

Topping:

½ cup sugar
1 cup orange juice
⅓ cup Grand Marnier
¼ cup slivered almonds, blanched

Combine all ingredients except almonds. Poke small holes in cake with a toothpick. Pour topping over hot cake in pan. Sprinkle with blanched almonds and let cool before removing cake from pan.

Join in the Fun at Our Membership Tea

Dodie Spell's Indian Summer Tea Punch
Date-Nut Finger Sandwiches
Olive Nut Ribbon Sandwiches
Chicken Salad in Finger Rolls
Cheddar Scones with Sliced Tomato
and Basil
Chocolate Dipped Apricots
Sweet Nothings
Lemon Truffles
Mocha Logs
Aunt Jessie's Cream Puffs

Dodie Spell's Indian Summer Tea Punch

Good anytime of the year

1 cup strong tea
1½ cups sugar
4 cups hot water
1 tablespoon almond extract

1 tablespoon vanilla extract
4 lemons, juiced
1 quart ginger ale

Make strong tea with 1 cup boiling water and 5 regular tea bags.
Let steep 10–12 minutes. Mix all ingredients except ginger ale in a
large jar. Shake or stir to dissolve sugar. Refrigerate to cool. Add
ginger ale and ice when ready to serve. May be served from a
pitcher or a punch bowl.

Cover fresh cut summer fruits with Sprite or mix with canned pineapple in its
own juice. The liquid keeps the fruit fresh for 3 or 4 days in the refrigerator.
Drain off juice to serve or remove portions with a slotted spoon.

Date-Nut Finger Sandwiches

Jo's grandmother's recipe

1 loaf thin sliced whole wheat bread, crust removed
1 loaf thin sliced white bread, crust removed
1 (6-ounce) package pitted dates, chopped
1 ¾ cups sugar
²/₃ cup light cream
⅛ teaspoon salt
2 tablespoons butter
1 cup pecans, finely chopped
1 cup mayonnaise

Trim crust from day-old bread. Combine dates, sugar, cream, salt and butter. Boil slowly, stirring constantly until dates have softened and mixture is thick. Cool.

Add nuts and mayonnaise. Spread date mixture on bread. Place another slice of the same kind of bread on top. Cut each sandwich into 3 rectangles. Makes approximately 90 small sandwiches. (Enough spread for 15 whole sandwiches).

Olive Nut Ribbon Sandwiches

Attractive on a tea table

1 loaf unsliced white bread, crust removed
1 loaf unsliced whole wheat bread, crust removed
Butter, softened
1 (3-ounce) package cream cheese, softened
½ cup pecans, finely chopped
½ cup pimento stuffed olives, finely chopped
2 tablespoons milk

Trim crust from the 2 loaves of bread. Cut each loaf horizontally into 6 slices. Mix the remaining ingredients, except butter.

For each ribbon loaf, spread each of 2 slices white and 1 slice whole wheat bread, first with butter then with ½ cup of olive nut filling.

Assemble slices into 3 loaves by alternating white and whole wheat slices. Top with unspread whole wheat bread. There will be four slices in each of the 3 loaves.

Cut loaves into slices about ½-inch thick (as if you were slicing bread to make a sandwich). Cut each slice crosswise into halves. Makes 3 loaves (10 dozen sandwiches); 1 cup spread.

Note: To freeze up to one month: wrap whole loaves well in plastic wrap, foil, then white freezer paper.

Chicken Salad in Finger Rolls

Ribbon adds a Victorian touch to an old favorite

1¾ cups cubed, cooked chicken breast
2 cups chicken broth (may use canned)
1¾ cups celery, minced
1 cup mayonnaise
2 tablespoons lemon juice
Salt and pepper
4 dozen tiny finger rolls
Ribbon

Poach chicken breast in the 2 cups chicken broth. Cool in the broth and remove skin and bones. Cut chicken into small cubes.

Combine cold cooked chicken and celery. Blend mayonnaise with lemon juice and add to chicken. Mix well. Season to taste with salt and pepper. Chill in refrigerator.

Cut finger rolls open on one side. Scoop crumbs from the center and fill rolls. Bind each with a narrow ribbon tied with a bow and floating ends.

If you would like, you could put deviled ham (on page 58) in half the rolls and tie them with another color ribbon.

Cheddar Scones
with Sliced Tomato and Basil

Bake in triangles and serve with jam, or in rounds with sliced tomato

2 cups all-purpose flour, unsifted
2 teaspoons baking powder
¼ teaspoon salt
6 tablespoons butter or margarine
1 cup sharp Cheddar cheese, shredded
⅓ cup milk
1 large egg
18 thin slices of fresh tomato
Fresh basil, chopped

Preheat oven to 425°. Combine flour, baking powder and salt. Cut in butter with a pastry blender until it resembles coarse crumbs. Stir in ¾ cup cheese. Combine milk and egg. Add milk mixture to dry ingredients. Stir lightly with a fork until mixture forms a soft dough. Knead gently 5 or 6 times on a lightly floured surface. Roll to a ½-inch thickness. With a floured 2-inch cutter, cut into rounds. Place 1-inch apart on a greased baking sheet. Sprinkle tops of scones with remaining cheese. Bake 12–15 minutes or until golden brown.

For directions on making triangles, see Lemon Scones on page 79.

Split rounds and serve with a cold tomato slice sprinkled with chopped fresh basil leaves. Makes 1½ dozen.

Chocolate Dipped Apricots
These go fast, so make a lot

3 ounces bittersweet or semisweet chocolate, chopped

30 dried apricots (about 5 ounces)

Melt chocolate in a small bowl over barely simmering water, stirring occasionally. Do not let water get into chocolate. Turn off heat. Keep chocolate over hot water for a good consistency. Dip each apricot, covering half. Let excess drip off. Place on foil lined baking sheet. Chill 10–15 minutes. Makes 30 confections.

Sweet Nothings
Fun to make

1 cup peanut butter
¼ pound (1 stick) butter or margarine
1 (12-ounce) package semi sweet chocolate chips

2 (12-ounce) boxes Rice Chexs
1 box confectioners' sugar

Melt first 3 ingredients in double boiler. Pour over Rice Chexs and stir to coat. Pour mixture into a brown paper bag with confectioners' sugar. Shake until coated. Place on cookie sheets, one layer deep to dry.

Lemon Truffles
Petite no-bake truffles that melt-in-your-mouth

¾ cup instant milk (in dry form)
2 cups confectioners' sugar
¼ cup sweet butter
¼ cup fresh lemon juice

½ teaspoon almond extract
½ cup pecans, finely chopped
¼ cup angel flake coconut, plus additional for rolling, (optional)

Mix dry instant milk and confectioners' sugar. Set aside. Melt butter over low heat. Remove from heat and stir in lemon juice and almond extract. Add sugar mixture, about ½ cup at the time, mixing until smooth each time. Add coconut, if using. Chill until firm enough to hold its shape. Roll into 1-inch balls. Roll in pecans or coconut. Chill until firm. Keep refrigerated until serving. Makes 2½ dozen balls.

Mocha Logs

Tiny chocolate-dipped logs have a sophisticated flavor

1 cup butter or margarine
¼ cup sugar
4 teaspoons instant
 expresso coffee powder
½ teaspoon salt
¼ teaspoon baking powder
1 egg

1 teaspoon vanilla
2⅓ cups all-purpose flour
8 ounces semisweet choco-
 late, melted and cooled
1½ cups pecans, finely
 chopped

Beat butter on high speed of a mixer for 30 seconds. Add sugar, coffee powder, salt, and baking powder. Beat until combined. Beat in egg and vanilla until combined. Beat in flour until just combined.

With a star plate of a cookie press, press dough in a 2-inch long strip onto an ungreased cookie sheet. Bake in a preheated 375° oven 10–12 minutes. Transfer cookies to a wire rack; let cool. Dip ends of cookies in melted chocolate, then in finely chopped pecans. Makes about 72 cookies.

Aunt Jessie's Cream Puffs

An old Natchez recipe that does not use eggs in the custard

Cream Puffs (page 51)

Pudding:
3 tablespoons cornstarch
⅓ cup sugar
⅛ teaspoon salt
½ cup cold milk

1½ cups scalded milk
1½ teaspoons vanilla
Powdered sugar

Mix cornstarch, sugar, and salt; combine with cold milk in the top of a double boiler. Gradually add hot milk, stirring until thick. Cover and cook over low heat 15–20 minutes, stirring occasionally. Add vanilla. Cool and fill puffs. Sift powdered sugar over the tops. Makes 24 miniature or 12 large cream puffs.

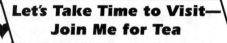

Let's Take Time to Visit— Join Me for Tea

Jayne's Lemon Raspberry Tea
Minted Cucumber Sandwiches
Curried Egg Sandwiches
Prosciuto Roses
Sander's Lemon Raspberry Squares
Banana Nut Tea Cake

Jayne's Lemon-Raspberry Tea

Serve in a pitcher or over ice in a punch bowl

16 cups water
10 tea bags
1½ cups sugar
1 (12-ounce) bag frozen
unsweetened raspberries

¼ cup fresh lemon juice
Fresh raspberries for garnish

Bring water to boil in a large pot. Remove from heat and add tea bags. Let steep 3 minutes then remove bags. Add remaining ingredients and let stand 3 more minutes, stirring occasionally, until raspberries thaw.

Pour tea through a strainer into a glass bowl or gallon-size plastic jug. Discard berries. Store in refrigerator up to 4 days. Serve over ice. Garnish with fresh raspberries. Makes 16 cups.

Vegetables that are to be served raw are best prepared the day before. Drain well, and place a layer of paper towels in the bottom of a heavy plastic bag. Close air tight and store in the vegetable bin of the refrigerator.

Minted Cucumber Sandwiches
Fresh mint adds a different taste

2 (3-ounce) packages cream cheese, softened
4 teaspoons chopped fresh mint

16 thin slices white bread, crust removed
1 long, thin cucumber, thinly sliced

Beat cream cheese with mixer until smooth. Beat in mint. Spread very thinly on bread. Cut each slice in half, forming 2 rectangles. Top half the rectangles with cucumber slices. Top with remaining rectangles. Makes 16.

Curried Egg Sandwiches
Different and delicious

3 tablespoons mayonnaise
1 teaspoon curry powder
½ teaspoon salt
¼ teaspoon freshly ground pepper
4 hard cooked eggs, chopped

6 tablespoons unsalted butter, softened
¼ cup chutney, chopped
16 thin slices whole wheat bread, crust removed

Combine mayonnaise, curry powder, salt and pepper. Stir in eggs. Cover and refrigerate.

In separate bowl combine butter and chutney. Cover and refrigerate.

Both may be refrigerated up to 24 hours. Before serving spread butter mixture on 16 slices of bread. Top half with egg mixture, then top with remaining bread. Cut sandwiches diagonally into quarters. Makes 32 sandwiches.

Prosciuto Roses

Beautiful as a canapé or tea treat

12 slices white bread
3 tablespoons unsalted
butter, softened

12 thin slices prosciuto
Flat parsley leaves

Remove crust from bread and cut into 24 rounds using a 1½-inch cookie cutter. Spread rounds with 1 tablespoon of butter. Broil in a preheated oven about 2 minutes, 2 or 3 inches from the heat until toasted. Cool on a rack.

Trim off fat edges of prosciuto. Cut each slice of prosciuto in half lengthwise, then fold each piece in half lengthwise. Stand slices on folded edge and roll up in a pinwheel.

Spread bread rounds with the last 2 tablespoons butter. Arrange prosciuto rolls with folded edges down on bread. Open petals of prosciuto at the top to resemble rose. Garnish with a flat parsley leaf. Makes 24.

Sander's Lemon Raspberry Squares

Delicious little yellow and red mosaics

CRUST:

1 cup flour
½ cup butter

2 tablespoons sugar

FILLING:

1 cup sugar
5 tablespoons flour
½ teaspoon baking powder

2 large eggs
4 tablespoons lemon juice
6 tablespoons raspberry jam

FROSTING:

1½ cups confectioners'
sugar, sifted
¼ cup butter

3 teaspoons lemon juice
(approximately)

To make the crust, mix the first 3 ingredients. Press into a 9x9-inch buttered pan. Bake at 350° for 30 minutes.

Sift together the sugar, flour, and baking powder. Beat eggs with lemon juice. Mix with the flour mixture and pour over the crust. With a teaspoon, dab raspberry jam into the batter at intervals, creating a mosaic effect. Bake at 350° for 25 minute. Remove from oven and cool.

Frost with confectioners' sugar that has been creamed with the butter. Add lemon juice to make a spreading consistency. Cut into 32 tiny squares to serve.

Banana Nut Tea Cake

A dainty two-layer prize-winning cake

2½ cups all-purpose flour
1⅔ cups sugar
1¼ teaspoon baking powder
1¼ teaspoon baking soda
1 teaspoon salt
3 eggs
⅔ cup buttermilk, divided
⅔ cup cooking oil

1¼ cups bananas, mashed
1 whole banana, sliced (for garnish)
1 cup walnuts, finely chopped, divided
1½ cups heavy cream
2 teaspoons sugar

Preheat oven to 350°. Grease and lightly flour 2 round cake pans.

Sift together flour, sugar, baking powder, soda and salt. Add eggs and ⅓ cup buttermilk alternately, mixing after each addition. With mixer slowly add oil, the remaining ⅓ cup buttermilk and the mashed bananas. Beat two minutes. Fold in ¾ cup walnuts. Pour batter into prepared pans and bake 35 minutes or until it test done. Cool on racks.

Beat cream until it holds soft peaks. Add 2 teaspoons sugar. Beat until it holds soft peaks again. Spread bottom layer of cake with ⅓ of the whipped cream. Top with the second layer. Spread top and sides with the remaining whipped cream. Arrange banana slices decoratively on top and sprinkle with remaining ¼ cup walnuts. Cut in small slices to serve.

PICNICS TO MAKE YOUR HEART SING

Ya'll Come! Bring the Family
to Celebrate the 4th of July

We'll Tailgate at the Usual Place—
Please Stop by

Let's Watch the Super Bowl—
An Indoor Picnic

A picnic is a mini-vacation, an escape from reality even if it takes place in your own backyard. Nothing could be cozier than watching the Super Bowl at a picnic by the fire or more exciting than traveling to the stadium to tailgate before your team's homecoming game. Nothing gives you that patriotic feeling like celebrating our nation's birthday at a star-spangled Fourth of July picnic.

With natural settings and happy occasions to put your friends in the mood, all you must do is provide plenty of robust food. There is something about a picnic that makes us extra hungry. Finger foods are the easiest to carry and serve, and it matters not a bit if they are messy. Just have lots of wipes and paper towels at hand. Top off your picnic with an array of fruits and lots of mouth-watering sweets.

Y'all Come!
Bring the Family to
Celebrate the 4th of July

Southwest Turkey Kabobs
Show-biz Tostades with Refried
Black Beans and Toppings
Peggy McKie's Salsa
Peggy's Guacamole
Tropical Fruit Platter
Alice Henderson's Creamy Corn Dip
Tray of Red, White, and Blue Desserts
(Strawberry and Blueberry Tartlets
and Cheesecake Bars)

Southwest Turkey Kabobs

An economical recipe that will serve a crowd

Marinade (below)
**3 pound turkey breast,
   boneless and skinless**
2 large yellow peppers

4 red onions
1½ pounds zucchini
⅛ teaspoon salt

MARINADE:

**2 tablespoons fresh lemon
   juice**
1 teaspoon salt
1 teaspoon garlic, minced
**½ teaspoon crushed red
   pepper**

¼ cup olive oil
**¼ cup fresh oregano,
   chopped, or 1 teaspoon
   dried plus ¼ cup fresh
   chopped parsley**

Mix together lemon juice, salt, garlic, and crushed red pepper; gradually whisk in oil. Stir in oregano.

Cut turkey into 1½-inch pieces (discard tough membrane). Toss turkey in the marinade to coat. Cover and refrigerate at least 4 hours (may be refrigerated up to 24 hours).

Cut peppers and onions into 1½-inch cubes. Cut zucchini into ¾-inch slices. Refrigerate, covered.

When ready to cook, thread turkey alternately on skewers with vegetables. Grill over medium hot coals, turning occasionally, 20 minutes or until done.

Show-biz Tostades
with Refried Black Beans and Toppings

Guests create their own masterpiece with toppings

**Corn tortillas (3 per person),
warmed**
**3 cups, plus cooking liquid
(approximately 27-ounces)
black beans, pinto or
kidney beans***
1 onion, chopped

2 cloves garlic, chopped
4 tablespoons butter
½ teaspoon cayenne pepper
**½ teaspoon ground black
pepper**
½ teaspoon cumin, ground
Wedges of lime for garnish

TOPPINGS:

**Black olives, green onions,
ripe tomato (chopped)**
**Lettuce and Monterey Jack
cheese (shredded)**

Jalapeno pepper (minced)
**Smoked oysters, guacamole,
salsa, sour cream**

Drain the cooked beans and reserve the liquid. In a skillet, combine the onion, garlic, butter and seasonings. Stir over medium heat to mix. Cover for 5 minutes over low heat until onion wilts. Uncover, turn heat to medium and add beans. With a large slotted spoon, roughly mash beans as you are heating them. They should be chunky and thick, retaining a little shape. Thin, if necessary, with some of the reserved liquid. Place in a bean pot and garnish with lime wedges to squeeze on beans.

To assemble: The crisp tortillas are warmed in the oven or fried in a skillet. (A half cup Monterey Jack cheese may be stirred into beans just before serving). Bowls of condiments are placed by the bean pot and guests serve themselves.

*Canned beans may be substituted.

Peggy McKie's Salsa

Homemade salsa is a wonderful treat

**2 (8-ounce) cans tomato
sauce**
½ cup cilantro, chopped
3 jalapeno peppers, minced
¼ medium onion, diced
**2 tomatoes, peeled, seeded
and diced**
1 stalk celery, diced
1 tablespoon olive oil

**2 garlic cloves, finely
chopped**
**1 dried hot chili pepper,
crushed**
½ teaspoon salt
**⅛ teaspoon ground black
pepper**
¾ cup water, approximately

Combine all ingredients except water. Add water gradually until desired consistency is reached. Chill. Keep refrigerated.

Peggy's Guacamole
A delicious chunky texture

Juice of 1 lime
2 large avocados, coarsely
 chopped
1 medium green pepper,
 finely chopped
2 tablespoons salsa
1 garlic clove, minced
1 large tomato, peeled,
 seeded, and chopped

1 celery stalk, minced
½ onion, minced
½ cup cilantro, chopped
½ teaspoon salt
⅛ teaspoon black pepper,
 freshly ground

Toss lime juice with avocado. Add the remaining ingredients. Mix. Do not make it too smooth. It should have a chunky texture. Place avocado seed in bowl with Guacamole. Cover and refrigerate. May be made several hours in advance.

Tropical Fruit Platter
Serve with a centerpiece of whole summer fruit for the children

1 (12-pound) watermelon
1 large fresh pineapple
4 kiwi fruit
3 papaya (cantaloupe may
 be substituted)
2 star fruit

1 head of California red
 lettuce
1 cup flaked coconut
1 cup granulated sugar
4 limes cut into wedges

Slice watermelon lengthwise into quarters and cut into 1-inch chunks. Cut the top from the pineapple (place cut side down on a large serving tray for decoration). Quarter pineapple lengthwise. Remove the hard core and discard. Cut pineapple into 1-inch pieces. Peel kiwi fruit and star fruit, slice horizontally. Peel papaya and slice lengthwise. Fruit will keep for at least 8 hours, if tightly wrapped, in refrigerator. Store each fruit separately.

Arrange the fruit on a large serving tray lined with lettuce. Scatter sliced star fruit over all. Put the coconut, sugar, and lime wedges in separate bowls. Guests add them as they wish. Serves 30 people.

Strawberry Snowdrops: Coat strawberries generously with confectioners' sugar leaving the hulls on for handles. Garnish puddings, pies and cheesecakes.

Alice Henderson's Creamy Corn Dip
Serve in a chafing dish

¼ pound (1 stick) butter or margarine

1 (8-ounce) package cream cheese, softened

1 (12-ounce) can white shoe peg corn, drained

1 (4-ounce) can hot chilies, chopped

1 teaspoon green Tabasco

Melt butter. Stir in cream cheese until smooth. Add remaining ingredients. Bake at 350° approximately 30 minutes or until bubbly. Serve with corn chips or rye crisps.

Strawberry and Blueberry Tartlets
Easy and you can prepare in advance

CRUST:

2 (3-ounce) packages cream cheese

²/₃ cup butter or margarine, softened

2½ cups all-purpose flour

½ cup ground almonds

Mix all ingredients and shape into 50 balls. Chill 15 minutes. Place in ungreased 1¾-inch muffin tins. Shape dough with fingers to make shells. Prick bottom with a fork. Bake at 450° 8–10 minutes or until they are brown. Remove from pan and cool on wire rack. Shells may be frozen in airtight containers up to one month. Let thaw before filling.

FILLING:

1 (3-ounce) package cream cheese, softened

1½ cups whipping cream

²/₃ cup confectioners' sugar

2 tablespoons amaretto liqueur

Beat cream cheese until light and fluffy. Add remaining ingredients. Beat until thickened. Cover and chill 8 hours or up to 4 days. Mixture will thicken when chilled.

To serve: Divide cream into shells and add fresh blueberries, raspberries or sliced or whole strawberries. Makes 50 tartlets.

Cheesecake Bars

A delicious, creamy bar cookie

CRUST:

1 cup all purpose flour
1 cup walnuts, toasted and
    finely chopped
⅓ cup light brown sugar,
    firmly packed

¼ teaspoon salt
⅓ cup butter or margarine,
    melted

Combine dry ingredients. Mix well with butter. Pat evenly into a greased baking pan. Bake 15 minutes in a preheated 350° oven.

CHEESECAKE:

2 (8-ounce) packages cream
    cheese, softened
¾ cup sugar

Grated peel of 1 lemon
3 eggs

Beat cream cheese, sugar, and lemon peel, until smooth. Add eggs, beating well. Pour over baked crust that has been cooled. Bake 25 minutes. Cool 5 minutes.

TOPPING:

1½ cups sour cream
3 tablespoons sugar

2 teaspoons vanilla extract

Combine ingredients. Spread evenly over cheesecake. Bake 5–7 minutes. Cool. Refrigerate at least 30 minutes. Cut into 1½x1-inch bars. Makes about 72 bars.

We Will Tailgate at the Usual Place—Please Stop By

Danish Lamb Loaf with Sweet Butter
and Black Bread
Crudite Bouquet with Yogurt,
Cucumber, and Garlic Dip
Pan Bagna (Italian Street Bread)
Tortellini and Artichoke Kabobs
Mexican Cheesecake
Picnic Potatoes
Mrs. Bookhart's Creole Chocolate
Cake Squares

Danish Lamb Loaf with Sweet Butter and Black Bread

Served thinly sliced, it is wonderful hot or cold

2 pounds lamb, ground
1 pound uncooked ham, ground
1 ½ cups soda crackers, finely crushed
2 eggs, well beaten
½ teaspoon salt
½ teaspoon ground black pepper

1–2 quarts beer (to cover loaf)

Garnishes:
 Picnic Potatoes
 Tiny pickled beets (commercial)

Mix the ground lamb and ham together. Add cracker crumbs, eggs, salt, and pepper. Blend thoroughly. Shape into a loaf or tube shape. Roll in a double thickness of cheesecloth and tie at both ends. Place in a pan on a rack (you may use an inverted saucer). Add enough beer to cover the loaf; bring it to a boil, cover and simmer over low heat for 2 hours. Remove from liquid, and refrigerate for at least 12 hours before unwrapping. Slice very thin. Garnish with picnic potatoes and tiny pickled beets. Serve with Danish black bread and unsalted butter, open faced.

Crudite Bouquet

Served in a basket, the vegetables make a lovely centerpiece

**Red lettuce, Italian parsley
and watercress
Assortment of fresh veg-
etables of choice for
dippers**

**Yogurt, Cucumber and Garlic
Dip
Long, thin loaves French
bread and Pita wedges**

Line a basket with lettuce. Fill in with parsley and watercress.

Tuck handfuls of prepared green onions, carrot sticks, green and red bell pepper strips, green beans, and fresh asparagus in hollowed out green, red and yellow pepper shells.

Nestle all in the lettuce-lined basket. Fill in with celery sticks and cherry tomatoes, or vegetables of your choice. Serve with Yogurt, Cucumber and Garlic Dip, crusty French bread and Pita wedges.

Yogurt, Cucumber and Garlic Dip

**1 (32-ounce) carton plain
yogurt
2 cucumbers, peeled,
seeded, grated coarse
3 garlic cloves
2 tablespoons olive oil**

**2 tablespoons red wine
vinegar
1 tablespoons fresh dill
White pepper to taste
Salt to taste**

Drain yogurt in a strainer set over a bowl, covered in the refrigerator overnight. Squeeze cucumber to remove excess liquid. Mix yogurt, cucumber, garlic, oil, vinegar, dill, white pepper and salt to taste. Serve with pita chips and vegetables.

Pita Wedges

Also wonderful sprinkled with herbs

**8 large Pita loaves
½ cup unsalted butter**

Salt to taste

Cut each Pita loaf into 8 wedges. Separate the wedges into 2 triangles. Arrange rough sides up in one layer on a cookie sheet. Brush lightly with butter. Sprinkle lightly with salt. Bake in a 375° preheated oven 10–11 minutes until crisp and gold. Make a day in advance. Keep tightly covered. Makes 128 wedges.

Pan Bagna

Means "bathed bread" sometimes called "Italian street bread"

1 (6 to 8-inch) round loaf of French or Italian bread
1 (6½-ounce) can light tuna in olive oil, undrained
1 2-ounce can flat anchovies in olive oil, undrained
1 tablespoon olive oil (approximately)
2 tablespoons red-wine vinegar
¼ teaspoon garlic, minced

1 (7-ounce) jar roasted sweet peppers, drained
5 red radishes, sliced thin
8 nicoise or other oil cured olives, sliced
¼ cup capers, drained
½ cup red onions, thinly sliced
1 tomato, sliced
3 scallions, white and green parts, cut in thin rounds

If you cannot find tuna and anchovies in oil, drain liquid from the cans. Place anchovies and tuna in a bowl and cover with olive oil. Cover and refrigerate overnight.

Drain olive oil from tuna and anchovies into a measuring cup. Add olive oil to equal ¼ cup. Add vinegar and garlic. Beat with a whisk until blended.

Cut bread in half horizontally. Spoon dressing over both cut sides. Place bottom half of bread on large plate. Spoon tuna on bread and arrange anchovy fillets over tuna. Top with layers of the remaining ingredients. Cover with other half of bread. Wrap loaf in plastic wrap. Return to plate. Place in refrigerator and cover with another plate. Place can or other weight on plate to press sandwich down. Leave 8 hours or overnight. To serve, let stand at room temperature 30 minutes.

Tortellini and Artichoke Kabob

A colorful and tasty appetizer

1 teaspoon cornstarch
1 teaspoon dried whole basil
1 teaspoon dried whole oregano
½ teaspoon sugar
½ teaspoon dry mustard
¼ teaspoon onion powder
¼ teaspoon garlic powder
⅛ teaspoon salt
⅔ cup water

½ cup cider vinegar
1 (14-ounce) can artichoke hearts, drained
24 cooked small spinach tortellini with cheese
24 cooked small cheese tortellini
12 small cherry tomatoes, halved

Combine the first 8 ingredients in a saucepan; mix water and vinegar and gradually stir it into dry ingredients. Bring to a boil;

Continued

cook 30 seconds, stirring with a whisk. Remove from heat and cool.

Cut 6 artichoke hearts into quarters. Alternate tortellini, cherry tomato halves and artichoke quarters on 24 (6-inch) skewers. Place in a baking dish and pour vinegar mixture over kabobs, turning to coat. Marinate in refrigerator 4 hours, turning occasionally. Drain and place on a serving platter. Makes 24 appetizers.

Mexican Cheesecake
A favorite with cocktails

2 (8-ounce) packages cream cheese, softened
1 (3-ounce) package cream cheese, softened
2 large eggs
2½ cups (10-ounces) Monterey Jack cheese with peppers
3 tablespoons green onions, chopped finely
1 (4½-ounce) can chopped green chilies, drained
2 tablespoons chili powder

1 teaspoon garlic powder
½ teaspoon ground cumin
1 (8-ounce) container sour cream
1½ cups thick salsa, medium hot
½ avocado
1 (4½-ounce) can chopped black olives
½ cup sweet red peppers, chopped
½ cup green onion tops or chives, chopped

Beat cream cheese until fluffy. Add eggs 1 at a time, beating well after each addition. Add cheese and next 5 ingredients, beating well. Pour mixture into a lightly greased springform pan. Bake at 325° for 30–40 minutes or until cake tests done with a toothpick. Gently run a knife around edges to loosen sides of pan. Remove sides of pan. Cool completely and chill.

Before serving, spread top with sour cream. Spoon salsa into a bowl and add ½ avocado that has been coarsely chopped. Stir. Place a tomato rose or some salsa in the center. Surround salsa with olives. Place red peppers around the olives then add a ring of green onions or chives. Spoon remaining salsa around edges. Serve with tortilla chips.

 Provide pots of good mustard as well as butter on the cheese tray. Swiss cheese is delicious with a strong mustard and goat cheese should always be eaten with butter.

Picnic Potatoes

A gala substitute for potato salad

18 tiny new potatoes, unpeeled
2 tablespoons mint leaves
1 cup mayonnaise
1 tablespoon prepared mustard
2 tablespoons chives, chopped

Boil the potatoes with the mint leaves, just until they are tender. They should still be firm. Drain and let cool to lukewarm.

Mix the mayonnaise with the mustard. Coat the potatoes with the mixture and sprinkle with chopped chives.

Keep chilled until serving time. Serve with toothpicks. Potatoes may be used to garnish the Danish Lamb Loaf.

Mrs. Bookhart's Creole Chocolate Cake Squares

It forms its own icing while baking

⅓ cup butter or margarine
1 cup sugar
3 tablespoons light cream
1 teaspoon vanilla
2 (1-ounce) squares unsweetened chocolate, melted and cooled
1 egg
1¼ cups sifted all-purpose flour
½ teaspoon baking soda
⅛ teaspoon salt
¼ cup water
½ cup semisweet chocolate pieces
½ cup walnuts or pecans

Mix shortening, sugar and cream until light and fluffy. Add in the vanilla and cooled chocolate, mixing well. Add the egg. Beat well.

Sift together flour, baking soda and salt. Add to the creamed mixture alternately with the water, beating after each addition. Spread mixture in a greased, lightly floured 9x9x2-inch pan. Sprinkle chocolate pieces and nuts over the top. Bake in a preheated 350° oven 30 minutes or until it tests done. Cool in the pan before cutting into 32 small squares and serving.

Join Us for the Super Bowl and an Indoor Picnic

Pork Tenderloin with Honey and
   Sesame Seeds
Hot Honey Mustard
   Mildred Brown's Crabmeat Quesadillas with
     Black Bean and Corn Salsa
    Cathy Taylor's Buffet Salad
     Norman Armstrong's Mississippi Sin
    Walnut Bourbon Balls
     Orange Almond Cheese Ball
      The Barnes' Orange Slice and Bake Cookies

Pork Tenderloin with Honey and Sesame Seeds

Serve with small buns and honey mustard

¾ pound pork tenderloin
¼ cup soy sauce
2 garlic cloves, sliced
2-inch piece of gingerroot,
   peeled and thinly sliced

¼ cup honey
1 cup sesame seeds

Place the pork in a heavy plastic bag. Combine soy sauce, garlic, and gingerroot. Pour over pork and let it marinate for 1 hour, turning several times. Drain and pat dry. Spread the honey on a plate and roll pork in it. Spread sesame seeds on another plate and roll pork, coating it completely.

Roast the pork in a roasting pan for 20 minutes in a 400° oven. Use meat thermometer in thickest part to be sure it is done.

Let the pork rest for 5 minutes and slice it thin on the diagonal. Serve with small buns or rolls with a bowl of honey mustard. Will serve 8–12 with cocktails.

Hot Honey Mustard
Give as gifts and keep some in the refrigerator

¾ cup dry mustard (2 ounces)   **½ cup honey**
¾ cup distilled white vinegar   **2 egg yolks**

Combine dry mustard and vinegar in a blender. Blend until smooth. Let stand overnight, covered, at room temperature.

Combine mixture, honey and egg yolks in a saucepan. Cook over low heat, stirring constantly until thickened (7–10 minutes). Cool. Refrigerate, covered, up to 2 weeks.

Mildred Brown's Crabmeat Quesadillas
Serve with black bean salsa for a feast

2 thin flour tortillas
Butter
1 tablespoon lime juice
2 tablespoons olive oil
2 thick slices avocado (approximately 1/6 of a small one or 1/8 of a large)
2–3 tablespoons fresh lump crabmeat, cartilage removed or

2–3 tablespoons grilled chicken strips cut into 4 or 5 pieces
1 tablespoon fresh tomato, finely chopped
2–3 tablespoons Monterey Jack cheese, shredded

This recipe makes one quesadilla. Multiply the recipe by the number of guests you plan to serve. For a long affair, men might eat 2 and ladies usually 1.

Butter one side of each tortilla. Combine lime juice and olive oil. Dip avocado in mixture; remove and mash lightly with a fork (should be chunky, not smooth). Spread on unbuttered side of tortilla. Sprinkle crabmeat over avocado. Scatter chopped tomato over avocado and sprinkle Monterey Jack cheese over all the ingredients (enough to cover completely). Place second tortilla on top, buttered side up (cook like you would a grilled cheese sandwich). Spray hot griddle or heavy skillet lightly with oil. Grill on one side 5 to 6 minutes. Mash edges down with top of spatula. Turn and cook the other side until cheese melts and tortilla is nicely browned. Cut into 6 to 8 wedges to serve.

Serve with any toppings desired and Black Bean Salsa.

Mildred's Black Bean and Corn Salsa

Mildred is a popular Jackson caterer

1 (14-ounce) can yellow corn, drained; or 4 ears fresh corn, cooked and cut from cob

1 (14-ounce) can black beans, drained and washed

½ red or sweet Vidalia onion, finely chopped

1 tablespoon jalapeño pepper, seeded and minced

¼ cup green pepper, minced

8 Roma or 4 regular tomatoes, finely chopped

3 avocados, finely chopped

¼ cup fresh lemon juice

2 tablespoons red wine vinegar

½ cup olive oil

2 tablespoons fresh cilantro, finely chopped

½ teaspoon coriander, ground

Salt and pepper to taste

Make salsa the day before you plan to serve it. Mix the first 7 ingredients together. Cover and chill. Whisk together the lemon juice, red wine vinegar and olive oil. Add the cilantro and coriander. Let stand at least 20 minutes. Gently stir mixture into the vegetables. Add salt and pepper to taste. Serve with crab quesadillas for a feast.

Cathy Taylor's Buffet Salad

A favorite with guests

⅓ cup olive oil

⅓ cup salad oil

1 cup red wine vinegar

1½ tablespoons sugar

1 teaspoon salt

1 large red onion, thinly sliced

½ cup celery, finely chopped

½ cup bell pepper, finely chopped

3 small yellow squash, thinly sliced

1 pint fresh mushrooms, sliced

2 (8-ounce) cans water chestnuts, sliced

2 (14-ounce) cans artichoke hearts, drained and quartered

12 slices bacon, fried and crumbled

1½ heads of broccoli, cut into florets

Mix oils, vinegar, sugar and salt. Mix remaining ingredients and toss with dressing. Marinate 4 hours or overnight, tossing often. Serve chilled. Serves about 20 people on an hors d'oeuvres table.

Norman Armstrong's Mississippi Sin

Ingredients are sinful, but the taste is divine

1 loaf round French bread
1½ cups sour cream
2 cups sharp cheddar
   cheese, shredded
1 (8-ounce) package cream
   cheese, room temperature

⅓ cup green onions,
   chopped
½ cup ham, chopped
⅓ cup green chilies, chopped
⅛ teaspoon Worcestershire
   sauce

Slice off top of bread and hollow out inside of loaf. Break scooped-out bread into 1-inch pieces. Lightly toast shell, top, and bread pieces in oven. Mix all other ingredients and pour into the hollowed-out bread shell. Place top on bread and reserve bread pieces for dippers. Wrap stuffed bread in foil. Bake in preheated 350° oven for 1 hour. Serve with bread dippers, plain crackers or chips.

Walnut Bourbon Balls

An old Southern favorite

2½ cups vanilla wafers
   (crushed)
1 cup confectioners' sugar
2 tablespoons cocoa powder
1 cup walnuts, finely
   chopped

3 tablespoons white corn
   syrup
¼ cup bourbon or rum
Confectioners' sugar for
   coating balls

Mix the first four ingredients well. Add syrup and bourbon; mix and roll into 1-inch balls. Roll in confectioners' sugar.

Orange Almond Cheese Ball

Serve this dessert cheese ball with orange cookies

2 (8-ounce) packages cream
   cheese, softened
4 tablespoons confectioners'
   sugar
1 tablespoon lemon rind,
   grated

1 tablespoon orange rind,
   grated
1 tablespoon orange juice
2 tablespoons orange li-
   queur
1 cup sliced almonds,
   toasted

Mix all except the almonds together into a ball. Roll ball in toasted almonds and chill. Serve with orange refrigerator cookies for spreading.

The Barnes' Orange Slice-and-Bake Cookies

A Natchez favorite

1 cup shortening
½ cup brown sugar
½ cup white sugar
1 egg
2 tablespoons orange juice
1 tablespoon orange rind, grated

2¾ cups flour
¼ teaspoon salt
¼ teaspoon soda
½ cup pecans, chopped finely

Cream shortening, add sugars gradually; add well beaten egg, orange juice and rind. Sift flour, soda and salt together and add. Stir in pecans. Form into rolls, wrap in waxed paper. Store in refrigerator until ready to use.

Slice thin, place on greased cookie sheets, bake at 375° for 12–15 minutes. Makes about 3 dozen small cookies.

INDEX

INDEX

INDEX

INDEX

"Best of the Best" Cookbook Series

Alabama	(28-3)	$14.95	*Mississippi*	(19-4)	$14.95
Arkansas	(43-7)	$14.95	*Missouri*	(44-5)	$14.95
Colorado	(84-4)	$14.95	*New England*	(50-X)	$16.95
Florida	(16-X)	$14.95	*North Carolina*	(38-0)	$14.95
Georgia	(30-5)	$14.95	*Ohio*	(68-2)	$16.95
Illinois	(58-5)	$14.95	*Oklahoma*	(65-8)	$14.95
Indiana	(57-7)	$14.95	*Pennsylvania*	(47-X)	$14.95
Iowa	(82-8)	$14.95	*South Carolina*	(39-9)	$14.95
Kentucky	(27-5)	$14.95	*Tennessee*	(20-8)	$14.95
Louisiana	(13-5)	$14.95	*Texas I*	(14-3)	$14.95
Louisiana II	(83-6)	$14.95	*Texas II*	(62-3)	$16.95
Michigan	(69-0)	$14.95	*Virginia*	(41-0)	$14.95
Minnesota	(81-X)	$14.95	*Wisconsin*	(80-1)	$14.95

Coming soon: **California, New Mexico, Plains States**

Individuals may purchase the full 26-volume set for a special "Best Club" price of $296.00 (a 25% discount off the regular price of $394.70 plus $8.00 for UPS shipping cost. Becoming a member of the "Best Club" will entitle you to a 25% discount on future volumes. Call for information on discounts for joining the "Best of the Month Club."

Other Quail Ridge Press Cookbooks

	ISBN SUFFIX
The Little New Orleans Cookbook (hardbound) $8.95	42-9
The Little New Orleans Cookbook, French Version (h/b) $10.95	60-7
The Little Gumbo Book (hardbound) $8.95	17-8
The Little Bean Book (hardbound) $9.95	32-1
Gourmet Camping $9.95	45-3
Lite Up Your Life $14.95	40-2
Hors D'Oeuvres Everybody Loves $5.95	11-9
Hors D'Oeuvres Everybody Loves II $7.95	91-7
The Twelve Days of Christmas Cookbook $5.95	00-3
The Complete Venison Cookbook (lay-flat paperbound) $19.95	70-4
Eat Your Way Thin $9.95	76-3
Kitchen Express (stand-up binding) $12.95	77-1
Best of Bayou Cuisine (lay-flat paperbound) $14.95	78-X

ISBN Prefix: 0-937552-. All books are combbound unless noted otherwise. Prices subject to change. To order, send check/money order to:

QUAIL RIDGE PRESS
P. O. Box 123 / Brandon, MS 39043
Or call toll-free to order by credit card:
1-800-343-1583

Please add $3.00 postage for any number of books ordered. Gift wrap with enclosed card add $2.50. Mississippi residents add 7% sales tax. All orders ship within 24 hours. Write or call for free catalog of all Quail Ridge Press books and cookbooks.